Sophia
Style

Sophia
Style

Deirdre
Donohue

FRIEDMAN/FAIRFAX
PUBLISHERS

A FRIEDMAN/FAIRFAX BOOK

© 2001 by Michael Friedman Publishing Group, Inc.

Please visit our website: www.metrobooks.com

Library of Congress Cataloging-in-Publication Data

Donohue, Deirdre.
    Sophia style / Deirdre Donohue
        p. cm.
    Includes bibliographical references and index.
    ISBN 1-58663-126-8 (alk. paper)
    1. Loren, Sophia, 1934-2. Loren, Sophia, 1934—Clothing. 3. Motion picture actors
and actresses—Italy—Biography. I. Title.

PN2688.L65 D66 2001
791.43'028'092—dc21
[B]
                                                                    2001023574

Project Editor: Hallie Einhorn
Editor: Alexandra Bonfante-Warren
Art Director: Jeff Batzli
Designer: Midori Nakamura
Photo Editor: Kathleen Wolfe
Production Manager: Rosy Ngo
Color separations by Bright Arts Graphics (S) Pte Ltd
Printed in Singapore by Tien Wah Press (Pte) Ltd.

1 3 5 7 9 10 8 6 4 2

Distributed by Sterling Publishing Company, Inc.
387 Park Avenue South
New York, NY 10016
Distributed in Canada by Sterling Publishing
Canadian Manda Group
One Atlantic Avenue, Suite 105
Toronto, Ontario, Canada M6K 3E7
Distributed in Australia by
Capricorn Link (Australia) Pty Ltd.
P.O. Box 704
Windsor, NSW 2756, Australia

dedication

This book is dedicated to my exquisite grandmother, Myrtle M. Hagan Repa, who always has been the style star of my life.

acknowledgments

Grazie, Signora Sophia Loren Ponti for being so elegant and so intelligent.

This book would not exist without Lee Stern, or the indomitable Alexandra Bonfante-Warren and Stéphane Houy Towner, or without Katell le Bourhis's indispensable role in my creative life. Project Editor Hallie Einhorn has been absolutely wise and tenacious every step of the way; Photo Researcher Kathleen Wolfe, assisted in her task by The Costume Institute Library, the Film Stills Library of The Museum of Modern Art, Time-Life, *Parade*, *McCall's*, and others, struck photographic gold. Generous and timely cooperation from both Violante Valdettaro at Valentino and Soizic Pfaff at Christian Dior produced many of the exhilarating finds in this rewarding treasure hunt.

I am humbled by my good fortune in having been the recipient of recollections and images from the splendid couturiers who have worked with Sophia Loren and those who still collaborate with her: Marc Bohan and Gianfranco Ferré were invaluable and brilliant contributors, as was Alexandre Barthet on behalf of his father, Jean. Edith Shaw Marcus and Meta Shaw Stevens were cheerfully openhanded with anecdotes and with exquisite, previously unpublished photographs by their gifted father, Sam. David Secchiaroli, likewise, made unique images by his father, Tazio, available to us.

One reason Loren is such a wonderful subject is that wonderful writing, both about her and by her, surrounds her. Biographies by Tony Crawley, Alan Levy, Stefano Masi, and Donald Zec, as well as, most recently, Warren G. Harris's thoughtful and thorough volume, all describe a winning woman from whom I have learned a lot.

The last word is for the beautiful people of style and substance who endured months of my Sophiamania: I thank husband Trevor Brown and the Donohues and Browns, Ann Butler, Minda Drazin, Dale Goldstein, Alexis Katz, Hermes and Katharine Knauer, Joan Lufrano, Doris Nathanson, Colleen O'Brien, Tasha Seren, Judith Sommer, Lynn Ann Underwood, and Bernice Weinblatt, as well as my big inspirations: Russell Bush, the Feuchtwangers, Harold Koda, Marilyn Lawrence, Caroline Milbank, Damon Powell, Martin Price, the Rands, the Robinsons, and Bonnie Rosenblum.

contents

Introduction   1

CHAPTER ONE: *Force of Nature*   11

CHAPTER TWO: *Earth Mother*   33

CHAPTER THREE: *Siren*   53

CHAPTER FOUR: *Diva*   71

CHAPTER FIVE: *Icon*   99

Selected Bibliography .114

Selected Filmography .115

Index 117

Valentino for
Sophia Loren 88

*S*ophia Loren is one of the world's most glamorous women and at the same time one of the most grounded. She wears big spectacles and sumptuous décolletages; has written cookbooks, a beauty book, and an autobiography; appears in her mid-sixties as a sexy Italian earth mother in madcap comedies; and makes films with cinema's most original directors as she approaches seventy. She has never been more beautiful.

Sophia Loren lives, as many film stars do, amid a montage of her movie roles, with still images filling in the spaces around them. Her image is both elusive and enduring, her style unique: assured, lively, all-embracing. This chronicle of her style encompasses the many different elements that seamlessly compose the elegantly complex Sophia Loren: not only her face and body—*that* face and *that* body—but her movement, her voice, her hair, her clothes, and, above all, her character.

One of the essential features of Sophia's style is her self-possession. There is nothing coy or conditional about the way she carries herself—she does not look for her reflection in the eyes or desires of others. Perhaps it is a legacy of the postwar years and of her intensely focused ambition, played out in the beauty contests and the unsentimental world of filmmaking, whether Cinecittà or Hollywood. Her body, once the means to her art, is an instrument of her art. Loren is perhaps at her most brilliant at film premieres, one of the best settings that moviemaking provides for its icons to appear before the public. She stands out on these occasions because of her height, opulent features, and bold tan in a sea of bony blondes (though she herself has been blonde at times), but even more because of her poised physical presence and her spectacular but genuine smile that expresses a larger-than-life joy.

Loren reevaluates her style on an ongoing basis, staying current and fresh. Helping to define the "super" in superstar, the retrospective palimpsest of images that is found in magazine spreads, book illustrations, and even gallery and museum exhibitions provides invaluable traces of her journey. At the same time, she is a person who has always lived in full public view, often under tabloid scrutiny, and she has always emerged beloved.

The biographical facts of Sophia Loren's life have often been reported. She was born Sofia Villani in Rome on September 20, 1934, to an unmarried couple—Romilda Villani, an actress and erstwhile semifinalist in a Greta Garbo–look-alike contest, and Riccardo Scicolone, a handsome engineer of somewhat aristocratic parentage. Sofia

OPPOSITE: Even in the early days, Loren had an iconic air about her. This shimmering look is the culmination of her fifties celebrity apprenticeship as an Oscar presenter, a trajectory also followed by Sophia's blonde counterpart, the luminescent Marilyn Monroe.

Scicolone (her father recognized her a few months after her birth) spent her childhood in Pozzuoli, a town just west of Naples. No less than their poorer neighbors, the family suffered the deprivations of World War II; the precocious Sofia closely observed the effects of poverty and how people survived. She took in all the hurly-burly ways and looks of the characters on the streets of Pozzuoli and Naples, and would draw upon this emotional material for her insightful performances.

In school, teachers remarked upon little Sofia's intelligence, but the scrawny twelve-year-old was known by the unflattering nickname *Stuzzicadenti*—"Toothpick." Soon, however, Sofia blossomed into a shapely, if shy, young teenager. Encouraged by her mother, Sofia resolved to take advantage of the opportunities presented by the postwar beauty contests, and at fourteen, she won a ticket to Rome. Mother and daughter set off to seek work as film extras in *Quo Vadis?* (1950), a Hollywood epic shooting at Cinecittà.

Sofia supported her mother and younger sister, Maria, by working as an extra and posing for the wildly popular *fumetti*, or photoplays, in which she was often typecast as an exotic vamp, no doubt because of her almond-shaped eyes and other Mediterranean features. She also modeled for a staggering number of pinup shots, which circulated throughout Europe, most often as postcards. She continued to enter beauty contests, often placing and always making a showing. One night when the still-teenage Sofia was dining out with friends, a judge for a beauty contest sent over an emissary who asked her to enter the contest. That judge was the successful producer Carlo Ponti, then in partnership with Dino De Laurentiis. The following day Ponti gave Sofia Lazzaro, as she called herself then, her first screen tests. They were less than promising, but she soon learned how to work with the camera. (And to this day, she forbids any shot of her from what she considers an unflattering angle.) Loren and the married but separated Ponti were soon a couple, ultimately finding themselves up against Italian law and the Roman Catholic Church in their attempt to marry. In the end, Giuliana Fiastri—Mrs. Ponti—would be the one to find the solution: all three parties would become French citizens, allowing the Pontis to divorce, and Sophia and Carlo to marry. (In her as-told-to–A.E. Hotchner autobiography, *Sophia Living and Loving: Her Own Story*, Loren referred admiringly to Fiastri as the best lawyer of them all.) Loren's fans followed her determined, and ultimately successful, efforts to bear children, the couple's two sons, Carlo Jr., known as Cipì, and Edoardo, or Pipo.

By 1959, Sophia had proven herself a gifted comic performer, as well as a dramatic actress to watch. Carefully guided by Ponti and through her own energetic efforts, Loren had signed a five-film deal with Paramount. Though she lived in Hollywood for only two years, 1958 and 1959, she made it into the winners' circle, the quintessential insider's

O P P O S I T E : Lord Snowdon's portrait of Sophia with her treasured, long-awaited first son, "Cipì," reveals her maternal affection and good humor.

event, presenting Oscars at both years' ceremonies. She would be on the receiving end in 1962, winning the first best-actress Oscar ever given for a performance in a foreign film.

In Hollywood, Sam Shaw became "Loren's photographer." At a time when U.S. producers tended to typecast her as a Latin spitfire, Shaw's handsome candids captured the reflective, independent woman who would soon emerge. Shaw, who had already taken his trusted lens to Marilyn Monroe with a profound sensitivity, turned the same attention to the inner woman-child of Loren. He was only the first of the great photographers and cinematographers who would contribute to Sophia's visual spell.

Her 1962 Oscar win officially elevated Loren to the rank of diva—the Hollywood Foreign Press Association gave her the Golden Globe for World Film Favorite in 1964, 1965, and 1969. She had graced a dizzying proliferation of magazine covers since her earliest cinema appearances, but *Vogue* offered celebrity of another order. Taken up by *Vogue*'s Diana Vreeland, Loren appeared on the magazine's covers and coveted inside spreads. On and off the set, she worked with the era's great photographers: Richard Avedon, Bert Stern, Neil Barr, Irving Penn, and Cinecittà's Tazio Secchiaroli.

Arabesque (1965), in the chic caper mode, played off Loren's fashion-diva status; nearly thirty years later, *Prêt-à-Porter* (*Ready to Wear*, 1994) confirmed it. Loren's association with fashion designer Marc Bohan of the House of Dior lasted for nearly three decades; he was to her what Hubert de Givenchy was to Audrey Hepburn. On- and off-screen, Loren has also worn Laroche, Balmain, Valentino, and Armani, and today she is a spokesperson for the Italian fashion industry. She has a brilliant gift for *inhabiting* her clothes, vivifying them so that they become eloquent extensions of herself or her characters, rather than mere coverings.

The 1960s also witnessed Loren's debut on the small screen. She made three television specials; taken together, they illustrate degrees in Sophia's progression from famous, attractive, and well-dressed Italian tour guide to Hollywood entertainer to international celebrity in the strictest sense: someone who is famous for being herself. Loren has a wonderful television presence; she establishes an immediate connection with her audience and conveys a feeling that she is sharing herself. Her warmth and amiability, with the suggestion that she does not take herself too seriously, is unexpected in an icon yet, paradoxically, fundamental to her public persona.

By 1980, Sophia Loren was well aware that her name was a "brand" that intimated powerful associations with her beauty, taste, and desirability. With the impeccable Loren-Ponti instinct for marketing, she also knew the value of keeping herself in the public eye, especially since she was in her mid-forties and entering the thinner air where fewer and fewer mature and classic actresses survive. In 1980, the hardworking star commenced her first entrepreneurial

OPPOSITE: Tazio Secchiaroli, like a wildlife photographer, shot the swooping figure of Loren between takes on the film *Arabesque*. That action picture was a perfect vehicle for the fit, couture-clad star, calling as it did for all kinds of physical activity.

venture, a name perfume with Coty. Even as she published her autobiography and starred in its television adaptation (as herself *and* her mother), she launched a signature line of eyeglasses, promoting them as a fashion item rather than a utilitarian device, and pitting her indisputable and intelligent sensuality and style against the received wisdom that glasses aren't sexy. Today, the large frames setting off her mesmerizing eyes—which she has claimed are her only particularly good features—are a permanent part of her look.

In recent years, Loren has received recognition not only for her work in films but also for her devotion to various humanitarian causes. Sophia Loren is an icon if anyone is—at a White House dinner, she was seated beside then-president Bill Clinton—but she is first and foremost a working actor. In 1994, she not only starred but dazzled in Robert Altman's *Prêt-à-Porter*, which played on her real-life role as a collection habitué who wears clothes more sensationally than any model. Shortly thereafter, in a return to her comic roots, Loren appeared in *Grumpier Old Men* (1995) with Walter Matthau and Jack Lemmon. She shines in a low-key role that combines her wonderful comic energy with her reputation as a fabulous cook. Loren shares the bill with Ann-Margret, and it is delightful to see two sex kittens of the 1960s still so alluring—not to mention employed—in ageist Hollywood.

Films, television specials, awards—all of these are the core of the Loren phenomenon, displaying her great talent, versatility, and charm. No one looks like Sophia—those eyes, that smile, that body, those gams that just won't quit, that defiant and sultry tan. But her style is much, much more. After all, neither her beauty nor her shape has ever really been in the prevailing mode. About her dissimilarity from waifs and androgynous sylphs, there is nothing to be said, and in the present era of hard bodies, she moves with a wiry strength that she has acquired over time. She is what women are traditionally not supposed to be: energetic, ambitious, in control. She has moxie; this may be what keeps her look consistent over time, regardless of the variations in hair and makeup. Always herself, she has never become a caricature of herself.

Sophia Loren is a manifold phenomenon made up of all the roles she has played in her life and in her art. She has the distinction of embracing elements of both baroque and Zen styles, in turn and together: baroque in her intimacy with the line beyond which lie kitsch and vulgarity—she revels in big hair and jewelry, opulent fashions, and all of the material goods that may compensate for her wartime penury, as well as in her boundless curiosity and humor; Zen in her focus on essentials—the minimum necessary for happiness—and in her love of her garden, the serious business of cooking, and her hard-won family. At the same time, an artist herself, she appreciates the evident hand of the artisan in her cultural milieu, from fashion to food.

O P P O S I T E : Signature Gianfranco Ferré for Dior *and* signature Loren: intricate lace illusion creates a suggestive and tantalizing effect that only accentuates Sophia's stunning poise at the New York premiere of *Prêt-à-Porter* in December 1994. A consummate sense of the occasion is a Sophia specialty, from the spectacles to the magnificent haute couture look.

The chapters that follow explore facets of the singular style of Sophia Loren. While her complexity—and the sheer number of images that exist of her—decree that her myriad aspects overlap, I have focused on five categories that together embrace this remarkable human being and her evolution: force of nature, earth mother, siren, diva, and icon. Because this is a study of a working actor, the dates given for all films are ones of production, rather than release.

$\sim$

A personal note: In the spring of 1954, the director Michael Powell dined with Ponti and Loren at the temporary Roman outpost of newlyweds Mel Ferrer and Audrey Hepburn. As Powell later described her in his 1990 memoir *Million Dollar Movie*, Loren "was a very large girl with gaps between her front teeth and a red dress gathered into a sash on one splendid hip. Standing with Audrey, who was tall and slender as a boy, they looked two different species . . . both of them collector's items."

That's the Sophia Loren I like best—the "collector's item." Yet I like her precisely because she is *not* some object on a shelf to be passively admired, but exactly the opposite: a large girl in a red dress animated by great intelligence. Further, I cannot help but love the extraordinary physical contrast between the two contemporary actresses who grew to be friends, neighbors, U.N. goodwill ambassadors, and stars in a rare firmament.

OPPOSITE: Tazio Secchiaroli, responding to Loren's complex and magnetic dedication to living, captured her irony as well as her expressive gestures.

Chapter One

Force
of
Nature

*L*oren, in her early Italian films, often seems to have just emerged from the Neapolitan slums. In fact, that captivating quality she has of being a force of nature translates into several overlapping styles: an earthy, independent-minded, and self-confident sex symbol; a folk-tale peasant with a touch of the ribald; the Hollywood version of the latter—the romantic, nonspecifically ethnic wench; and a fierce survivor drawing on deep inner resources.

The force-of-nature character that Sophia perfected in many of her films also manifested itself in the beginnings of her real-life career. She had, almost from the start, an instinctual understanding of the effect of both her body and her Neapolitan ethnicity. Sophia played this persona to good effect with the press, which ran with the semi-myth of her gritty beginnings and her rise to stardom as the creation of the urbane Milanese producer Carlo Ponti (in the role of Pygmalion). Many fan-magazine articles, for example, "revealed" how Sophia's supposedly rough demeanor was being polished by her new celebrity. Then there is the related matter of her dialect. When she arrived in Rome in 1949, Sofia Scicolone spoke with such an impenetrable regional accent that her earliest films were dubbed—into Italian! Before she mastered all of the languages she now commands—Italian, French, English, German, and Spanish—Sophia first had to perfect her Italian, or, more specifically, her Roman, the accent of film stars like Anna Magnani. Such hurdles contributed to her audiences' perception of her as provincial and even, erroneously, rural.

La Loren's great appeal to international film audiences lay, at first, in the implicit sensuality of the tousled, apparently unself-conscious way her characters wore their hair, their seeming lack of makeup, and their disheveled or carelessly worn clothes. Those looks mirrored a deeply traditional society blown apart by war and a rapidly changing culture. For many U.S. cinema audiences of the 1950s, the gritty neorealist representation of Sophia and others may have provided respite from the self-contained, gloved, and stockinged postwar but prefeminist American woman.

Sophia Loren's energy, even today, is fearsome; the intensity with which she portrays her survivor characters—whether comic or dramatic—evokes a ferocity that has, on more than one occasion, inspired comparisons with other species. When asked by *Newsweek* in 1955 what the American fascination with Italian actresses was all about,

PAGE 10: Lord Snowdon's photographs of Sophia possess the dignity and poise of his royal portraits. But the direct gaze and straightforward sensuality are trademark Sophia Loren. OPPOSITE: *C'era una volta (More Than a Miracle)* features Sophia as a tatterdemalion heroine. In the natural cotton layers of her fairy-tale weeds, she looks like a prototypical hippie.

Clemente Fracassi, who had directed Loren in *Aïda* (1953), said it amounted to "the call of the wild." The headline on the cover of the May 6, 1957, issue of *Life* magazine trumpeted Loren as a "Tiger-Eyed Temptress."

At the same time, Sophia and her characters often manifest, to different degrees, that highest of human attributes: self-awareness. (This Chinese-box consciousness of acting a part, even as she plays it, recalls some of the wry works of another southern Italian cultural treasure, the Sicilian playwright Luigi Pirandello, who won the Nobel Prize for literature the year Sofia Villani was born.) In life and in film, she undermines and overturns the rigid strictures of conventional society, bringing a seductive depth to her dramatic roles and resonance to even her lightest comedies.

*I*n the comedies, Sophia's vibrant survivors triumph within the anarchic, subversive world of women maneuvering within and sometimes manipulating the rules of the dominant patriarchy. She has played irrepressible roles almost from the first, both exploiting and transcending her physical attributes in outfits ranging from drenched tatters to peasant costumes. Mistress of the natural acting style, she conveys spontaneity in every gesture, making her uniquely suited for the deft tongue-in-cheek humor of *commedia all'italiana*.

The best of these Italian comedies combine laughter with a sense of desperation, reflecting the characters' struggles to survive in the face of overwhelming obstacles. Irony, the grotesque, and the cynical Italian vision of life were very different fare from the Hollywood movies in which Loren's contemporaries were starring, although the picturesque poverty seen in the more sentimental of the Italian films tended to include a *povera ma bella* (poor but beautiful girl), whose unsocialized sensuality provided both good humor and visual interest. Loren's ability to embody the Dionysian types of peasants and other earthy roles was more a function of studious observation than of her own background or wartime deprivation. She is a supple and subtle actor, as well as a good mimic, while her intelligence and wit prove her to be neither diamond-in-the-rough nor victim.

Recognizing the spirit and tough street smarts that Sophia was able to communicate through her talent and her unusual good looks, producer Carlo Ponti and director Vittorio De Sica channeled her into such felicitous early vehicles as *L'oro di Napoli* (*The Gold of Naples*, 1954). Loren's personal style, evident in her bearing, combines determination in the face of chaos, humor in the face of absurdity, and seemingly indomitable vitality. These qualities made her perfect for her role in *L'oro di Napoli*, which was an "omnibus" film based on a book of short stories by Giuseppe Marotto, a Neapolitan writer. In the film, Sophia stars in an episode titled "Pizza a credito" (Pizza on Credit) as a fetching pizza-seller named Sofia. Sporting a white off-the-shoulder peasant blouse, she takes a long, unforgettable walk in the rain, knowing that *her* appeal

OPPOSITE: Sophia Loren and Carlo Ponti have proved to be an enduring and powerful team. The complementary smiles seem to validate Sophia's contention that she was "born married to Carlo."

is not to be found in demurely arranged clothes and coiffure. While De Sica recognized that Sophia was perfect for the role of the *pizzaiola*, he had to convince Ponti's coproducer, Dino De Laurentiis, to hire the nineteen-year-old novice for the part.

It was *L'oro di Napoli* that projected Sophia Loren's image outside Italy and linked her inextricably with the peasant blouse and its multifarious sexual connotations. The peasant blouse is "natural," which means (theoretically) braless; titil-latingly precarious in its perch on the bust and shoulders, the peasant blouse suggests sexual accessibility. (The most famous Hollywood peasant blouse was created by Howard Hughes, who drew upon his considerable engineering skill to construct a bra that suggested the verisimilitude of being braless for actress Jane Russell in *The Outlaw* [1938], which he directed.)

Fashion designer Marc Bohan obtained his first impression of the star who would later be his client at the House of Dior when he saw *L'oro di Napoli* upon its release in Paris. Although her role was not large, Loren radiated a lumi-nous, magnetic presence that Bohan has compared to Marilyn Monroe's. Loren's natural force before a camera depends not on narrative, clothing, or cinematography, but on her profound humanity and inner beauty.

The Naples of 1680 was the setting for *La bella mugnaia* (*The Miller's Beautiful Wife*, 1955), a comedy that brought together Marcello Mastroianni, De Sica (as an actor), and Loren, who plays Carmela, the title character. Based on the Pedro de Alarcón play *El sombrero de tres picos* (*The Three-Cornered Hat*), the film garnered an enthusiastic reception. In this "petticoat-and-peasant-blouse" picture, Sophia spends most of the time not in an actual peasant blouse but in a more revealing corset cover. She works the petticoats to great visual advantage with a flurry of activities that keep them flying.

That same year, director Dino Risi's *Pane, amore e . . .* (*Scandal in Sorrento*, 1955), the first all-Italian produc-tion in color and CinemaScope, again paired De Sica, as an actor, and Sophia. The film presented La Loren as a vocal fishwife known locally as "the Heckler," but the wildest part of her uninhibited performance is a mambo that she per-forms with great abandon. Loren's would-be peasant garb and vivaciousness aroused manly sentiments in the U.S. press; one representative comment was from *The New York Times*'s A.H. Weiler: "Much of the film's footage is a vivid illustration that Signorina Loren in a tight bodice or writhing through a mambo dance in a low-cut flaming red gown is likely to raise the temperature of any red-blooded citizen."

The peasant blouse of *Pane, amore e . . .* is improbably detailed and unpeasantlike, featuring lace trim, decora-tive flounces on the shoulders, and lingerie buttons down the front (the top one is open). Loren's harsh makeup; black, shaped Mephisthophelean eyebrows; and piled-up hair contribute to a very stylized and theatrical character, not out of keeping with the new, somewhat overbright CinemaScope process. Nevertheless, Sophia overcame the limitations of costume, makeup, and artificial film color with her usual robust good humor and charismatic moves.

O P P O S I T E : Carmela, the robust Neapolitan peasant in *La bella mugnaia*, capitalized on the demand for more Sophia in more peasant blouses.

In 1961, exploiting a successful formula, *Boccaccio '70* and *Madame Sans-Gêne* (*Madame*) further explored a celluloid peasant-style Sophia Loren. The big names associated with the former, beginning with the fourteenth-century Italian writer Giovanni Boccaccio, included the directors—De Sica, Luchino Visconti, and Federico Fellini—who each helmed an episode. Mario Monicelli directed a fourth episode, which was edited out of the version released in the United States.

In the episode titled "La Riffa" (The Raffle), Loren plays Zoe, a woman who works in the shooting gallery of a traveling fair in the Po Valley of northern Italy. To make the money she needs to support her extended family, she offers herself as the top prize in the weekly raffle. *Time* magazine's review found time for a fashion report:

> *In an outgrown red dress, her hair a disheveled beehive, dripping fresh honey, she laughs and smirks and races the blood of the aged. A big bull gets loose and panics the fairground, thundering and charging through the crowds. The animal stops and takes a long fierce look at Sophia. She slowly removes her blouse. The bull stands glazed for a moment, then runs off snorting in inexplicable terror....*

Sophia's *Boccaccio '70* dress is a tongue-in-cheek combination of sexy gypsy and contemporary fashion, which she carries off with pouting aplomb. The bodice has a vertical row of fringe down the center and the implication of a drawstring over the bust, but surrenders all pretense of the picturesque by the time it reaches the waist. The narrow, above-the-knee skirt reflects the height of fashion while testifying to the star's exceptional figure and famously long legs.

Madame Sans-Gêne, based on the play by Victorien Sardou and Emile Moreau, tells the story of Catherine Huebscher, the laundress and vivandière whom Napoleon raised to duchess of Danzig. The film boasts Loren as the scrubbed and boisterous protagonist in an opulently décolleté peasant blouse. The costumes for the film were designed by Marcel Escoffier and Italo Scandariato, who created truly detailed historical Napoleonic court dress for the later scenes. For most of the film, however, the laundress's drawstring muslin blouse and layers of skirts are her featured wardrobe, which Loren wears to good effect for her scripted frolicking and revolutionizing.

C'era una volta (*More Than a Miracle*, 1966), directed by Franco Rosi (another Neapolitan!), provided Sophia with another opportunity to play the rags-to-riches fashion story; the tagline for the film was "A fairy tale about a peasant girl who, after a series of misunderstandings, comes to marry a prince." Set in Naples in the 1600s (like *La bella mugnaia*), the film inspired critic Vincent Canby of *The New York Times* to give this fashion commentary:

> *She does spend most of the picture in one of those break-away peasant mini-dresses in which she first burst upon the public consciousness. During one sequence, Sophia is entirely hidden in a barrel, which is just another example of how Mr. Ponti has squandered his natural resources.*

OPPOSITE: Among the local products displayed and purveyed in a country fair is Zoe (Loren), an Amazon in a red dress with kinetic bead fringe. This episode of *Boccaccio '70* features Loren in a coy update of her many peasant roles.

Everything that Loren wears in the film (except the barrel) was designed by the costumer Giulio Coltellacci. The assertively ragged edges of her careworn costumes are visibly artistic, evidently created through no small effort. Nevertheless, the sheer beauty of the wardrobe, however distressed by stagecraft, maintains the film's fairy-tale quality.

By the time the film was released, there was something in mainstream fashion that looked unmistakably like a wild version of Sophia Loren's peasant style. The flower children had been discovered by the general public and by fashion magazines, and designers adapted and glamorized their rag-bag folk-fantasy costumes. These designs were a sign of the times, exhibiting naturalism, freedom, and a romanticism about the past.

The Sophia Loren peasant role that is possibly the least naturalistic is that of Aldonza in *Man of La Mancha* (1972). There is dirt all over her, but her costumes were steadfastly conceived with her character—and her shape—in mind. She is the ultra Hollywood wench. Luciano Damiani designed both the costumes and the sets for the film. While not strictly historically accurate, the clothing retains the handmade quality of thick, rough, unfinished garb and is appropriately dramatic and exaggerated. The almost frenzied hair and makeup are as stylized as the costumes, but it is a slicker Sophia who sports them. *Time* magazine's Jay Cocks remarked in 1972 that "she seems to be playing a kind of high-stepping version of *Two Women*." It is unclear whether this disquieting comment alludes to the rape scenes in the two films or to the thick socks and torn bodices that characterize both ensembles.

*I*t is in her dramatic films that Loren most breathtakingly explodes on the screen as a force of nature—complex, enduring, and ultimately indomitable. The first of these dramas to gain international attention was *La donna del fiume* (*Woman of the River*, 1954), intended to be a vehicle for Sophia's sensuous earthiness. The intriguing story behind the making of *La donna del fiume* reveals something about the competitive cooperation that operated in the De Laurentiis and Ponti star-making venture.

In 1949, Giuseppe De Santis's film *Riso amaro* (*Bitter Rice*), about the exploitation of workers in the rice fields of the Po Valley, launched nineteen-year-old Silvana Mangano—De Laurentiis's protégée, lover, and future wife—into the stratosphere as a sex symbol. The film was an international success for the team, so when Ponti discovered the promising and shapely teen Loren, he already had a notion of how to exploit her natural magnetic quality.

La donna del fiume, a postneorealist melodrama set among the exploited poorest of the poor in northern Italy, casts Sophia as a girl in an eel cannery who ultimately ends up cutting cane at the mouth of the Po River. She sports ill-fitting shorts, rustic sweaters, and sun hats—and she owns the screen. The masculine attire only emphasizes her

O P P O S I T E : Aldonza, Cervantes's antiheroine in *Man of La Mancha*, although related to Loren's earlier peasant roles, is artfully alluring and decoratively bedraggled.

raffish charm—her strong, long legs in gum boots project almost a cartoon effect of a big, beautiful country lass, while her male-laborer work shorts are rolled up as far as they can go. Although Sophia was intended to be a nubile bit of visual compensation, she took advantage of the opportunity to showcase her burgeoning acting ability.

Nature meets her match in the Sophia of Jean Negulesco's *Boy on a Dolphin* (1956), La Loren's ultimate wet-look film (see pages 24–25). Negulesco, a Rumanian painter turned director and screenwriter, had been around Hollywood for some time. By the time he started *Boy on a Dolphin*, his repertoire of visually sophisticated films included *Humoresque* (1946), *Johnny Belinda* (1948), and *How to Marry a Millionaire* (1953), but it was *Three Coins in the Fountain* (1953) that made Italy fashionable again. This romance about three American girls, set against postcard-pretty Roman backdrops, was a successful attempt to transfer the formula of *How to Marry a Millionaire* to another scenic locale. The unexpected result was a tourist boom in Rome and a taste stateside for all things Italian, including clothing, fine art, and cinema.

Boy on a Dolphin capitalized on the Italy craze by showcasing Loren (even though she played a Greek woman). In his autobiography, *Things I Did. . . and Things I Think I Did*, Negulesco, stoking the public's belief in a Sophia Loren "in the rough," gave the following account:

> The shoes were uncomfortable; they were her enemy. At the first shot where her feet were out of view, she took them off. She suddenly became free, secure with the dignity of a peasant. She looked radiant and noble. I thought to myself, if she could always remember to take off her shoes, to be free Sophia with no rules, with no makeup, no acting tricks, she could become a legend.

Loren obligingly provided the press with the myth that she was the real thing, referring to herself as a miraculous rags-to-riches Italian peasant. This romantic notion was perfect fuel for the Hollywood publicity machine, however much the facts might have been otherwise. At a welcome party for Sophia at Romanoff's—hosted by 20th Century Fox, which was releasing *Boy on a Dolphin*—gossip legend Hedda Hopper reported of her, "Perfectly enchanting—and very tired. If she weren't such a strong healthy peasant, she would have collapsed."

Shortly after the release of *Boy on a Dolphin* came *Desire Under the Elms* (1957). Delbert Mann's film version of Eugene O'Neill's hit play was retrofitted to Loren by the Italianization of the lead female character. The costumes achieve a balance between handmade and "realistic" on the one hand, and the height of Victorian romanticism on the other. In fact, *Look* magazine compared Loren, wearing these outfits, to Greta Garbo in *Camille* (1936). The comparison holds best in the way that the two wardrobes romanticize poverty, placing more emphasis on a fashion-plate silhouette than on a scarcity of materials, the undesigned look of handmade garments, or other relevant details.

OPPOSITE: Nives, the woman of the river to which the title *La donna del fiume* refers, is a soggy, but irrepressible heroine, whose pinned and rope-tied clothes accentuate her natural expressiveness—and earthy humor. This ironic publicity shot plays on Loren's own already sophisticated commodification.

*I*t is easy to understand why screenwriters and directors commenced drenching the teenage Sophia Loren in her films. Long before Bo Derek and Jacqueline Bissett got soaked on their way to stardom, there was a Venus on the half shell who inspired film audiences at least as profoundly. It's not a new formula, but there is certainly something inexplicably modern about the Loren mermaid.

Sophia, an avant-garde combination of sensuality and nature in her wet roles, was unashamed of getting revealingly dunked as part of the action in her movies. The active role, in fact, has always been her forte, so it is not passive exploitation of her physique that motivates the wetness, although many viewers consider the result a bonus. Whether she is swimming or caught in a spray, Sophia all wet is as characteristic a guise as Sophia in a peasant blouse.

For Loren, it all began with *Africa sotto i mari* (*Africa Under the Seas*, 1952), a dramatic narrative layered onto documentary footage. It was her first feature role, and according to her autobiography, she did not know how to swim until the first day of shooting—when she was thrown in the water! Little did she know the experience was just the beginning of nearly a decade of wet appearances onscreen.

Loren, as a character named Sofia in De Sica's *L'oro di Napoli* (*The Gold of Naples*, 1954), performed a long, slow stroll through the pouring rain—an arduous sequence for the actress, who contracted bronchial pneumonia and had to stay in bed for a month after shooting concluded. No sooner had she recovered than *La donna del fiume* (*Woman of the River*, 1954) started filming. The movie featured the young Loren in a tight, wet shirt and shorts that shrank provocatively in the drying sun.

Pane, amore e . . . (*Scandal in Sorrento*, 1955) featured the soaked Donna Sofia, a fishwife, who is thoroughly splashed with seawater in the commission of her fish-market tasks. The character graced the cover of the August 22, 1955, issue of *Life* magazine. It is rather startling to imagine this overtly sexy photograph on 1955 American coffee tables, as Loren is wearing an elaborate peasant blouse with black trim *soaked to her body*.

In *Boy on a Dolphin* (1956), Loren played a Greek sponge diver named Phaedra. No one would have predicted that the film would live forever primarily as a pinup of a sopping Sophia in a clinging yellow dress—no one, that is, except Jean Negulesco, the director. The account of the

ABOVE: The early, amphibious Sophia roles featured unspectacular dress, taken from men or from mundane work-ing attire and thoroughly soaked. In this still from *Boy on a Dolphin*, Sophia provides the visual missing link between Esther Williams and the Bond girls.

yellow dress in his autobiography is thoughtfully detailed: a photograph that he had seen of a Japanese pearl diver suggested the idea for Phaedra's costume—a plain cotton dress, tied with an old cord, that came up between the legs like a diaper. Negulesco even test-soaked it:

> After the first dunking, an explosive image appeared, with every detail of Sophia's perfect body outlined dangerously. Per-haps too dangerously for the film censors, so I took the dress back and had it dou-ble-lined. The second dunking gave us the sensual suggestion, but without the obvious lusty truth. Exactly what I wanted.

As a point of comparison, the Alfred Hitchcock film *Vertigo*, released almost a year after *Boy on a Dolphin*, featured Kim Novak being fished out of the bay—not only dry but still coiffed and made-up. Clearly, the Negul-esco experience was exceptional, lying beyond the industry standard.

Recollecting the early days of her career for *Life* magazine in 1960, Loren quipped, "It seems I spent the first five years in movies hav-ing people throw pails of water over me."

The prevailing mid-nineteenth-century shape is especially flattering to Loren's height and natural hourglass figure; she is well served by corsets and crinolines. While the layers of petticoats hide her long legs, they also multiply the animation of her movements. Her character in O'Neill's drama is dark, unpredictable, and impossible to rule, yet her costumes are sweeter and more ordinary. Edith Head, the chief of costume design for Paramount at the time, assigned the challenging design for this moody historical picture to Dorothy Jeakins. Jeakins, who had started as a sketch artist at Fox in 1938, was now the gold standard of theatrical cinema costumers, having graduated from Paramount's stable to do *South Pacific* (1957), among other hits. In 1965, she would be nominated for an Academy Award for her designs for *The Sound of Music*.

Desire Under the Elms is visually notable for what seems to be the first zealous application of body makeup since Sophia's performance as an African in *Aïda* (1953). In the film, Sophia sports a heavy tan, intended to suggest outdoor labor, wildness, and Mediterranean exoticism; it is a look that works with the part. However, the use of body makeup became a point of contention in Melville Shavelson's *Houseboat*, made the same year. Loren's costar, Cary Grant, was dismayed by her liberal use of body makeup for the role of Cinzia, a woman of high social status and wealth. To him, and to Hollywood, these characteristics translated to a fair complexion—for a woman. However, Sophia, adhering to Italian cultural norms, believed that a maximum suntan was a sign of wealth and conspicuous leisure. The result was not as jarring to the viewer as it was to the precisely elegant Grant, mainly because it was the norm for passionate "Latin" characters to be as dark as Loren is in the film. It was only one of the first cultural differences in style that Loren and Hollywood would have.

Loren's wasp waist was also featured in the first film in which she performed in English. *The Pride and the Passion* (1956), a Stanley Kramer historical epic filmed in Spain, featured Frank Sinatra as a Spanish revolutionary named Miguel, Loren as a camp follower named Juana, and Cary Grant as an English Royal Navy captain, Anthony Trumbull. Sinatra and Loren depict Hollywood-style exotics, complete with Sophia's seductive Spanish dance, in which she moves with such showstopping voluptuousness that she makes the moment a wonderful set piece of the film.

Although Loren is camping along the Spanish countryside with the rebel troops, she manages a few wardrobe changes. For the most part, she is clad demurely in full peasant skirts, with wide belts to set off her small waist, and very tailored peasant bodices. Variations include a ruffled décolletage and layered petticoats, complemented by strappy sandals. All in all, it is uninspired western señorita drag from Hollywood, where Mediterranean and Mexican were apparently interchangeable. At the same time, the above silhouettes, with their full skirts and cinched waists, also echoed familiar 1950s fashion.

OPPOSITE: Rural 1850s New England provides the backdrop for the imaginative, romantic wardrobe of Loren's character in *Desire Under the Elms*. In keeping with the Italianization of Eugene O'Neill's original character, homespun costumes were supplemented with exotic chiffon.

The film's costume designer, Joe King, was a studio wardrobe person and designer throughout the 1950s. He designed the costumes for Billy Wilder's *Witness for the Prosecution* (1957), *Judgment at Nuremberg* (1961), and *Guess Who's Coming to Dinner?* (1967). The romanticism of *The Pride and the Passion* is tempered by the palette, which is earthy and not at all "Latin," except for the use of black.

The makeup was designed by a Hollywood veteran, John O'Gorman, whose vast résumé includes such epics as *Around the World in Eighty Days* (1956), *Dr. No* (1962), and *The Curse of the Fly* (1965). The challenge in *The Pride and the Passion* (as in the other pictures on which O'Gorman worked) was to meld fantasy and reality—not to mention cross-ethnicity and messy action—without obscuring the actors' celebrated physiognomies. Grazia De Rossi styled Loren's hair, creating a look that is uncharacteristic of the Italian actress: curly, with bangs, perfectly charming and youthful. The epic was only De Rossi's second film, but she would go on to serve as hair designer for Loren in two films by Anthony Man, *El Cid* (1960) and *The Fall of the Roman Empire* (1963).

*I*n one of her most memorable screen images, Loren, dirty, exhausted, and unkempt, crouches on a dusty road, weeping. The shapeless, filthy dress she wears is torn at the shoulders; her legs are stuck into coarse, droopy socks; her hair is a whipped mop; her face and arms are streaked with mud. With De Sica's *La ciociara* (*Two Women*, 1960), based on Alberto Moravia's best-selling and controversial 1957 novel of the same name, Loren earned the first Oscar ever conferred on an actress for a foreign film. The role of Cesira, a refugee mother fleeing first the Germans and then the Allies in the Ciociaria region of Italy, had been intended for Anna Magnani, with Loren as her daughter. Magnani turned down the part because she felt that, at fifty-three, she was too young to portray Loren's mother; she challenged De Sica to cast Loren as the mother instead. De Sica did so, despite his reservations that Sophia was, at twenty-five, too young.

Elio Costanzi—the film's art director, production designer, and costume designer—worked for less than a decade on the Italian film scene, often on British or American productions shooting in Rome. This was the only project on which he worked with Sophia Loren, and it was his most important film. The look of the film is raw, with an arid quality throughout. In keeping with the production design, Sophia's wardrobe and makeup achieve an almost documentary level of realism.

Although Loren has said that De Sica compelled her to play the role without the benefit of makeup, the film's credits include a name that recurs in Loren's force-of-nature personifications: Giuseppe Annunziata. He is credited as the makeup artist for such movies as *Matrimonio all'italiana* (*Marriage, Italian-Style*, 1964), *C'era una volta, La mortadella* (*Lady Liberty*, 1971), and *Man of La Mancha*. These films, by a variety of directors in a number of different

O P P O S I T E : This silk interpretation of nineteenth-century Spanish peasant dress is more informed by Loren's appealing shape than by 1820s dress styles, just as Juana, a revolutionary in *The Pride and the Passion*, is more about movement and seduction than history.

locations, share a common denominator in the effect of the makeup, a painterly interpretation of grime and/or "the school of hard knocks" that is aesthetic and at the same time contributes to the dramatic narrative. The height of make-up design is exercised in such films: film convention requires Sophia Loren to have enhanced lips and fully fringed eyelashes with mascara, while at the same time conveying a realistic, even bleak image. In *La ciociara*, the overall muting of the makeup, along with the shadows around her large eyes, makes her a picture of unadorned, primal power.

Stripped of the appearance of makeup in *La ciociara*, Sophia went spectacularly straight. With her hair looking as if it had been stirred with a stick and her famous long legs (but not her equally famous bosom) disguised in floppy dresses, she turned in a ferocious performance that attracted universal acclaim. As a wartime rape survivor and the anguished, fierce mother of a raped thirteen-year-old child, Loren surpassed everything she had done in her thirty-five preceding pictures.

The ragged, war-ravaged film character was an arresting counterpoint to the movie-star persona she had perfected by 1961. Vincent Canby recounted in *The New York Times* the response that greeted the U.S. premiere of *La ciociara*:

> *The lights came up on her in the audience, and there was this most beautiful woman in a dress cut down to the navel looking ravishing. She had been on the screen as this tattered, worn, raped survivor of war, and the contrast just sent the audience into hoots of applause.*

OPPOSITE: This famous shot from *La ciociara* captures the power of Loren's Oscar-winning performance. Even in this split second, all of the legendary actor's tools come into play—gesture, emotion, natural womanliness, and stature.

Chapter Two

Earth Mother

*W*hen Alberto Moravia wrote the novel *La ciociara*, the Ciociaria region of Italy, south of Rome, was one of the poorest in the country. Cesira, the archetypal mother in a land famous for its *mammismo*, or mother-worship, is a primordial fury in her single-minded, almost savage focus on her daughter, Rosetta. Cesira, an uneducated woman from a profoundly traditional, almost ageless culture, displays a range of motherly feelings and behaviors, from gentle delight to terror to a frantic urgency as she pleads for justice on her daughter's behalf. Appalled at her daughter's loss of "honor," appalling as she screams her daughter's intimate violation to the heavens and to passersby, Cesira is bewildered and helpless before the sea change in her child, just as she is unaware that the war and its aftermath have transformed her world forever.

This wrenching emotional and physical portrayal of a mother and of motherhood was turned in by a twenty-five-year-old actress previously known for her elemental sex appeal, whether in comic parts (what Sophia once called "confectionary roles") or dramatic ones. So convincingly profound was Loren's performance that the actress found herself denying rumors that Moravia had written the book about her and her mother, although she acknowledged that she had drawn on her mother's response to wartime deprivation.

Sophia may have drawn on more than that. Her own mother, Romilda Villani, was glamorous, urbane, and, as Loren herself observed, discomfortingly beautiful. Villani was anything but an earth mother, as unlike the prototypical Neapolitan *mamma* as anyone could be, though Sophia affectionately called her by the fond diminutive *Mammina*. Nor was the extended Scicolone family a conventional one. With a stunning, image-conscious mother; a dapper, uniformed grandfather; and a handsome though absent father, they bore little resemblance to the rest of Pozzuoli's families. Nevertheless, the reality of motherhood is, of course, more various than often depicted. While Villani may not have been the matronly, black-clad figure in the family kitchen, she did set aside her own dreams of Cinecittà to become a *madre ambiziosa di teatro*, or stage mother, on behalf of her elder daughter. Loren has always cited her relationship with her mother as being the fulcrum for her life: the two were very close, and Villani's own independence and struggle for identity probably provided the necessary stimulus for Sophia Loren, the actress and woman.

PAGE 32: A fashionable, babushka-wearing Sophia was photographed in her splendor for the publicity campaign for *I girasoli* (*Sunflower*, 1969). Loren is all modish glamour, though promoting an unglamorous heroine. OPPOSITE: Mother Nature's darling: Sophia captured by Lord Snowdon, in what is quite a departure from the airless settings of his royal portraits.

What is antithetical to an earth mother if not a movie star? A public figure deals in a more or less artificial persona, while the female principle embodies the essential, internal soul. As always, however, Loren, the woman to whom Vittorio De Sica paid tribute in a 1962 *Vogue* magazine portrait as "spiritually honest," is the exception, reconciling apparent opposite qualities with conviction, as well as with a characteristic blend of grace and frankness.

Undoubtedly, the honesty Loren brings to her roles works both ways, illuminating parts of herself *to* herself. Onscreen, she is the earth mother extraordinaire. With keen insight and precise physical gestures, she portrays the inner existences of the most humble of women—women who are anything but forces of nature.

The quality that Sophia Loren has perfected is an ineffable ability to transform the mundane domestic life of women into singular, supremely poignant portraits. Perhaps she owes this skill, in part, to her childhood; not having experienced the vernacular structure of a "normal" Italian home life, she may have been able to see the mythic potential of the quotidian. It may be, too, that the absence of a father in her crucial growing-up years, and in such a patriarchal time and place, permitted her a freedom of expression she might otherwise never have known. When Moravia interviewed Loren in 1962, he made much of this psychological basis for her success.

The Black Orchid (1958) features Loren as an Italian widow, Rose Bianco, with a son in reform school; she is being wooed by an uncharacteristically mild-mannered Anthony Quinn. Martin Ritt, the director, knew what he had. He told journalist Donald Zec: "Here was this all-powerful woman playing a woman who was left with a child, supposedly mature, experienced and a widow, yet Sophia was clearly in the bloom of her late twenties!" In fact, Loren was not yet in her mid-twenties. She was rewarded with the best-actress award at the Venice Film Festival—and a greatly enhanced professional credibility.

Edith Head designed a Hollywood interpretation of Italian émigré widow's weeds for the picture: 1950s soap-opera style. In the film, Sophia dons low black pumps, black calf-length dresses with lace trim, scarves for church, and plaid aprons for the home front. She seems to radiate from within the austerity. Far too pretty for the flat hair and loosely cut coats, she looks positively liberated at the end of the movie in her bridal gown, which is far more appropriate to her unlined face. Fortunately, such dowdy fashions were not characteristic of her Hollywood contract years. Head, chief designer at Paramount from 1938 to 1967, didn't miss a chance to sign her name at least once to designs for most of the big stars during that prolific period. This was one of three films in which she and Loren worked together directly, *Houseboat* (1957) and *Heller in Pink Tights* (1959) being the other two.

OPPOSITE: *Even as a contrite widow in* The Black Orchid, *Loren never manages to hide her light under a bushel. Swathed by Edith Head in suitably matronly black and lace, Loren nevertheless remains indelibly appealing.*

In *Houseboat*, a film made to capitalize on the splendid screen chemistry Loren and Cary Grant had generated in *The Pride and the Passion* (1956), Sophia plays a rebellious escaped socialite named Cinzia, who discovers her inner earth mother with the aid of Tom Winston, a widower with three rowdy children. Loren's conventionally "Italian" look in the film no doubt goes far in winning her the hearts of the whole brood—Cinzia is a classic Italian babe who sings, dances, and cooks. This is signature American Loren, in one of the most beloved of her U.S. films. She is chic, and her fashions show her off to her best advantage, a bathing beauty and a glamour-puss all in one. Unlike her character in *The Black Orchid*, she reveals much leg—in a bathing skirt slit to the waist—and all of her gowns make the most of her hourglass body.

It Started in Naples (1959) again offers us Sophia as a little bit earth mother and a little bit siren. In a kind of pastiche of her screen roles to that point, her performance shuttles between Madonna and Magdalene in this most obvious, even black and white, of manifestations—a broad Hollywood kind of costume "capriccio," on the island of Capri.

The sense of place that pervades Sophia Loren's onscreen identity is essential to her earth-mother roles. She has often acknowledged the importance to her of her Neapolitan identity, and she draws on her childhood experience in creating these roles. In fact, so poor was her family that even though the world-famous island of Capri lies just off the coast of Naples, Loren's first visit there was with Clark Gable for *It Started in Naples*.

In the film, Loren manages to appear in consecutive scenes with rag-rolled hair, in a blue cotton housedress and apron, and then, as a nightclub performer, in a green-sequined leotard with violet streamer skirt. The duality of her character, Lucia Curcio, is conveyed by gestures as well as dress: the Italian housewife, with hands on hips, gazes heavenward in exasperation, while the sexy performer wiggles suggestively in a risqué dance. Both attitudes are encompassed by the timeless pageantry of Naples. In the courtroom, fighting for custody of her nephew, Lucia is dressed modestly in black with white neck covering, the picture of purity. (In a sarcastic response to her onscreen play-acting, Clark Gable asks Vittorio De Sica, in the role of his attorney, "Who won the Academy Award this year?")

Orsetta Nasalli-Roca created the contrasting wardrobes, infusing them with a great deal of fantasy: the giant pockets and the plackets and collars are almost like a childhood expression of both motherhood and sexuality. All of Sophia's looks in the film are bold and colorful, in keeping with her almost farcical interpretation of the roles.

The energy of *Matrimonio all'italiana* (*Marriage, Italian-Style*, 1964) derives from a perfect blending of motives that few actors could have integrated as seamlessly as Loren. Based on the hugely successful play *Filumena Marturano* by Neapolitan Edoardo De Filippo, the film depicts a decades-long relationship between Domenico (Marcello Mastroianni) and Sophia's character, Filumena, a whore *and* a mother. In an understated example of virtuoso acting,

O P P O S I T E : The role of Madonna/Magdalene so well suited Loren's range and beauty that she took it on in a number of films, including *It Started in Naples*.

Filumena ages more than twenty years, gradually trading the conventional trappings of sexuality for the plain, matronly dresses of domesticity. Filumena's internal odyssey is effected through more than costume changes, however: Sophia somehow projects a physical alteration over time, her body becoming more centered and at the same time more fatigued, drawing on deeper and deeper resources to achieve her end—her children's well-being. No longer externally an official object of lust, Filumena nonetheless feels desire and love for Marcello Mastroianni's character, Domenico Soriano, adding another dimension to the marital scheming urged by her powerful maternal drive. It did not hurt her performance to be playing opposite Mastroianni, who specialized in characters of a self-centered, infantile, and evasive nature—perfect foils for Loren's all-woman women.

In the first episode of the Oscar-winning *Ieri, oggi e domani* (*Yesterday, Today and Tomorrow,* 1962), Loren portrays the complex maternal feelings of an ostensibly "simple" character, Adelina, a black marketer who repeatedly gets pregnant to take advantage of the maternity deferments mandated by the law but eventually ends up in jail. Regardless of her original motivations, Adelina's maternal feelings surge to the surface, and Loren in the crowded common cell with her smallest children in tow and offering her breast to her newest baby is a heart-wrenching image. The prison scenes were shot on location in Naples, with actual prisoners on hand during the filming. After the picture had wrapped, Loren received a note from one of the prisoners that said, "God will bring a real baby to bless your life, beautiful lady."

Indeed, this powerful performance was delivered by a woman who, at the time, had no children of her own. But La Loren has always been a professional, spinning her acute observations, even those remembered from her childhood, into cinematic gold. In her autobiography, *Sophia Living and Loving: Her Own Story,* she recalled the time when Peter Ustinov, her director for *Lady L* (1965), complimented her on her portrayal of a pregnant woman, despite her lack of personal experience of the condition. Sophia retorted that she had seen pregnant women "in the streets for fourteen years of my life!"

The tabloid-reading public in Italy was well aware of Sophia's unsuccessful and heartbreaking efforts to have children of her own. Loren's compassion and understanding of the souls and struggles of the most disenfranchised of her compatriots, as well as her often-voiced loyalty to her background, seem to have evoked a reciprocal affection and concern. As she noted in her autobiography: "Because I'd been portraying human and natural characters—peasants, mothers—the contradiction that I wasn't able to have children of my own made people very upset." Ultimately, after years of disappointment, she gave birth to two sons, Carlo Jr. in 1968 and Edoardo in 1973. Hers were among the most minutely media-scrutinized pregnancies of modern times—and few new mothers have ever been more glamorous.

OPPOSITE: The inherent styles of Mastroianni and Loren worked together so well that De Sica paired the actors in three different ways in *Ieri, oggi e domani* (here, in the episode "Adelina of Naples"). In every case, Loren commands and Mastroianni submits, but somehow he defines her.

Again and again, Loren's own strong maternal instincts have inspired almost awed comments. Intrepid still photographer Tazio Secchiaroli, Loren's de facto documentarian, suggested that perhaps her best earth-mother impulses are so spontaneous and profound that they evade being recorded; he recalled one such instance: "Immediately, Sophia stood in the doorway spreading her dress so that the baby wouldn't get the draft. It was so staggeringly beautiful, and I was so taken aback by the sight of it that I completely forgot that I had a camera in my hand."

*I*n her first film after the birth of Carlo Jr., Loren was reunited with De Sica and Mastroianni. *I girasoli* (*Sunflower*, 1969) is almost an Italian-Russian folk tale. Its characters are gloomy and brooding, and nature seems to play a role of its own; Sophia Loren in the middle of a field of sunflowers in the Ukraine is an indelible image. Her character, Giovanna, is outfitted in both a modern version of folk dress—consonant with the peasant look of 1960s fashion—and generic matronly dress. The designer was Enrico Sabbatini, a master of historical and biblical epics and an almost fifty-year Cinecittà veteran who worked with Loren on a number of pictures.

I girasoli was challenging because there was the hope that it would be a female version of *Doctor Zhivago* (1965), which Ponti felt justly proud of having produced; however, for an epic, its time span is vaguely contemporary, and its venues, for the most part, lack grandeur. Thus, there is great emotional, even operatic, emphasis on the heroine's looks. Indeed, she comes across like an international folkloric-industrial peasant. In terms of visual sophistication, *I girasoli* is a radical departure from Loren's premotherhood films. Her character has, in effect, digested both Cesira from *La ciociara* and the zeitgeist of the 1960s, and indicates the direction in which De Sica and Loren would take her style.

Once again, Loren plays a woman whose story is followed over an extended period of time; this time, she progresses from siren to aging loner. The film suffers from an uncertainty in direction that Loren attributed to the dark passage that only female actors pass through: as post-ingenues and pre-dowagers they are hard to pigeonhole. And yet this is precisely the obstacle that Loren has overcome time and time again in magnificent portrayals of "ordinary" aging women. The contrast between actress and characters is all the more remarkable in that the full-blown, vibrant Sophia Loren tends to make more rather than less of her physical attributes: she wears her hair large; she accents her fabulous eyes with dramatic makeup, thick eyelashes, and huge glasses; and with frank self-awareness, she opts for fitted bodices and styles that show off her long, shapely legs.

Costumes, hairstyles, and makeup all play a distinct and important part in the films in which Loren ages and downplays her sensuality—films that are, in a sense, vehicles for Sophia's tremendous talent for physical acting.

O P P O S I T E : In *I girasoli*, Loren's character, Giovanna, wearing layers of paper-sack-colored and -shaped garments, despairs of ever discovering the fate of her MIA husband (Mastroianni).

*W*hether mussed or coiffed within an inch of its life, Sophia Loren's hair has always been a phenomenal part of her style. And it is at its most impressive when oversize, to balance the ample features of her face, her long neck, and her tall, shapely body. In the 1960s, legendary *Vogue* editor Diana Vreeland was mad about an abundance of hair, and Loren had it!

Sophia has obviously been experimenting with her hair for a long time. Indeed, as an actor, she knows how to use its expressive power to maximum effect, with eloquent gestures such as the toss of a head, a bouncing mane, or a long lock falling mysteriously over an eye. Loren describes in *Women & Beauty* how the radically dissimilar hairstyles in *Madame Sans-Gêne* (*Madame*, 1961) helped her to carry herself in each of the character's two distinct aspects: a washerwoman, then the duchess she becomes. The contrast was between the apparent *absence* of a hairstyle and a very tight and rigid one, so the physical sensation must have been antipodal.

In Lina Wertmüller's *Francesca e Nunziata* (2000), Loren wears tight curls with swaths of gray throughout. It is startling to note that the style is somehow age-appropriate yet so unlike Loren's own silky hair. The harsh frizziness of her hair as Francesca is reminiscent of her hair for her first film with Wertmüller, *Fatto di sangue fra due uomini per causa di una vedova* (*Blood Feud*, 1978). It is a southern Italian look, with a harshness and realism that match Wertmüller's very different personal female expression; Wertmüller has always worn her white hair in a no-nonsense shorn style.

Sophia was featured in a 1963 international edition of *Hairdo* magazine especially for her infinite variety of hairstyles. Providing more behind-the-scenes information than movie stars of the time generally did, she was candid about the fact that not only was her own hair styled in a variety of ways, but she often wore wigs and hairpieces to keep her hair healthy. Such devices were a wise alternative to assaulting her follicles with the changes in style and color required by her vastly different roles.

In fact, she frequently indulged in the Hollywood mania for variety in coiffures through the application of false hair. She delighted in being a platinum blonde in *Heller in Pink Tights* (1959) and an eighty-year-old in *Lady L* (1965), as well as in having mounds of hair in a number of roles such as *El Cid* (1960) and *Desire Under the Elms* (1957). In every case, she divested herself of the wig, fall, or other piece at the end of each day's shooting to emerge refreshingly clean and contemporary.

In *Women & Beauty*, Loren calls hair "the vital accessory." She proves to be undidactic but detailed about its care. Naturally, given her origins, she recommends the practice of combing olive oil through the hair and sitting in the sun for an occasional deep-conditioning!

Loren notes that hair is identity and that one can influence one's identity by changing one's hair. At the same time, she decries hair that is unsuitable, uncomfortable, or labor-intensive, saying, "You should have a style that makes you feel at ease no matter what the weather, the time of day or the wind velocity."

LEFT: Loren's ceaseless variety of coiffures, particularly in the 1950s, included many unlikely looks.

Formless dresses with unfitted waistlines, skirts to the knee or longer, unmade-up eyes, and limp, tightly confined hair enhance these audacious and moving characterizations; Loren's women become worn, their wills countering their profound fatigue or illness in roles from which other glamorous actors would flee.

Not all of Loren's women are working-class, though. *The Voyage* (1973), the last film that Vittorio De Sica directed, is a costume picture based upon a novel by Luigi Pirandello. Set in Sicily, Naples, and Venice in 1912, the film features Loren as Adriana De Mauro, a Sicilian widow with a heart ailment. Her love interest is her late husband's brother, played by Richard Burton. The widow's costumes were designed by Marcel Escoffier. Although the movie takes place during the enchanting fashion period preceding World War I, the costumes are often dour in color, pattern, and upholsterylike detail; nonetheless, they're elegant and dripping in minute particulars. Escoffier, one of the most accomplished European historical designers, was well known to Loren, having previously worked on her costume pictures *Madame Sans-Gêne* (*Madame*, 1961) and *Lady L.*

A year later, Burton and Loren teamed up again in a Hallmark Hall of Fame production of Noël Coward's *Brief Encounter*, which aired on NBC. This time both characters were drab, suburban, and married—and Burton and Loren were accordingly more subdued in their acting and dress. This is the kind of role that convinced Sophia Loren, approaching the age of forty, to move forward with provocative, challenging, and unbeautiful work that was entirely more satisfying than many of the comedies and "epics" in her past.

Loren approached director Ettore Scola, who specialized in delicately limned political films, to create an unconventional pairing for her and Marcello Mastroianni. *Una giornata particolare* (*A Special Day*, 1975) cast Sophia Loren as Antonietta, the weariest and meekest of housewives, and Mastroianni as Gabriele, a homosexual. The time is 1938, the year Mussolini promulgated the racial laws that forbade Jews to work in the public sector. The occasion—the "special day"—is one of Mussolini's obligatory spontaneous demonstrations, this time in honor of a visit by Hitler. Both Loren and Mastroianni are sitting the flag-waving out, each for individual reasons. Some critics were uncomfortable with the unexpected characters, while some praised them; all of the participants considered it their best work. The costume designer was Enrico Sabbatini, here working on an unusually intimate canvas.

Antonietta is rumpled, faded, and unkempt; she has dark circles under her eyes and a long-neglected mop of hair. She is in many ways the weakest female of Loren's career, yet her triumph is that she survives to make dinner for her family at the conclusion of the film. She is perhaps one of the most moving of Loren's Italian-housewife heroines, and the film's historical emphasis points to the timeless quality that many of those roles share.

OPPOSITE: In *The Voyage*, Loren—as a sublime Sicilian widow in the waning moments before World War I—wears handmade Italian linens evocative of her character's domesticity and interiority.

*T*n 1990, Loren starred in her third film based on a work by Edoardo De Filippo—this time, a novel. Lina Wertmüller directed her in *Sabato, domenica e lunedì* (*Saturday, Sunday and Monday*), a comedy set around the weekly ritual of *ragù alla napoletana*, which requires making the Sunday dinner on Saturday; the story takes the viewer from the preparation of the meal through the Monday aftermath. Loren plays the matriarch and central domestic authority. By this time, her earth-mother roles had practically made her the patron saint of the Italian kitchen, and her dear, soft, shapeless print dress and modest, graying cap of hair are seemingly archetypal evocations of home. Of course, the narrative is not so simple, since the perceptive De Filippo hardly had a one-dimensional take on Neapolitans.

Sophia Loren had been making two and three films a year since the mid-1950s; by 1970, she was an established star, her public style a byword for gorgeousness. Suddenly, in 1971 (1972 in the United States) she projected an entirely new public image. *In the Kitchen with Love*, Loren's first cookbook, is as redolent of Neapolitan humor, life lessons, and domestic tradition as its bountiful dishes are of the southern sun. The cover, composed like a Renaissance portrait, depicts her amid a cornucopia of natural ingredients, her chin resting on her hand in an equally natural gesture of warmth and contentment. With no irony, Sophia wears a classic smocked and embroidered peasant blouse, matched with a full, colorful, patterned skirt and apron. Inside, photographs portray her performing household chores, including squatting among chickens in the yard and throwing pizza dough in the air. One might smile at such images of over-the-top, almost stereotyped Italian domesticity coming from one of filmdom's most hardworking actors, who is a devoted mother and businesswoman besides. Yet these photographs express a profound part of Loren's personality and, if not the experience she had, at least the experience she wishes she'd had. Furthermore, they come across as manifestations of her joy in motherhood, a literal celebration of nurturance, and a way for Sophia to share cherished family pleasures with her public.

Food and cooking provide metaphors for several aspects of Sophia Loren's life; for example, her nicknames for people are the dishes she associates with them, either because of their evocation or preference: for Carlo Ponti *involtino*, for other intimates *zeppolo* or *frittata*. Her second cookbook, *Sophia Loren's Recipes & Memories* (1998), weaves together stories about her life and career with related recollections. Many of her memories of cooking hark back to her domestic inspiration, her grandmother—Nonna Luisa—forcefully creating something from nothing in her kitchen in Pozzuoli during the hardest of times. In the art of cooking, as in the art of acting, Sophia insists that everything must be *genuino*—natural. She brings a joviality to the kitchen and to her digressions that is basic and unaffected.

O P P O S I T E : Photographer Sam Shaw captured the extracurricular domestic goddess, a young Sophia Loren, frying eggplant in Hollywood.

Loren discussed her craving for a conventional hearth and home with Alberto Moravia in a 1962 interview for *Show* magazine: "My biggest [complex] was that I did not have a normal family . . . meaning a real father who lived with us and took care of us and worked to support us and a real mother—I would have preferred her to not be so beautiful and to be a real mother instead—the kind they have in Pozzuoli, who are old and even ugly." Sophia pursued her dream in public for decades, first defeating obstacles to marry the man she loved and still loves, then to bear children. At the same time, she has a wider notion of family, forming close-knit professional relationships that have endured, grown, and deepened with time, as well as the temporary but intense connections born on film sets. In August 1962, Loren told *Life*, "I hate to finish a picture. It means everyone goes away, just like breaking up a family."

This is the same Sophia who has appeared on magazine covers and at galas dressed to the nines in opulent gowns by the best couturiers, who are privileged to enhance her assets magnificently. Within that public peacock brilliance there lives a private, devoted mother, not only to her children, but to herself—the *mamma* Sophia that keeps her warm and well fed and makes sure that she is a good person. Both *genuina* and self-created, Loren has found the inner truth of her lifetime dream. With her usual openness, she has reported as much: in a September 2000 interview, Barbara Walters suggested, "Your story, you have said, what you became, is really what your mother wanted to become." To which Loren responded, "I think so. . . . I think she's the real Sophia Loren. . . . My mother is Sophia Loren."

OPPOSITE: Was womanly virtue ever so lovingly—and chicly—personified as in this vision of Sophia knitting? Interviewed by *Life* in 1961, Loren challenged, "What does beauty mean, after all? There must be more than that, something inside."

Chapter Three

Siren

*T*hrough whatever multifaceted perspectives Sophia Loren is viewed today, it would be disingenuous to downplay her impact as a sex symbol. While she has achieved excellence in her acting skills, her physical appeal is an essential part of her identity—a part that she herself recognizes. Approaching her sexuality with acceptance and good humor, she has been refreshingly frank about her allure, its exploitation, and its significance to her as an actress and a person. "I'm not ashamed of my bare-bottomed beginnings," she has repeatedly told interviewers. Indeed, she was notoriously unashamed of being photographed in a variety of seductive poses early in her career. The money, of course, was needed, and she was able-bodied.

Early on, Ponti and Loren shrewdly converted an Italian cinematic tradition into 1950s Hollywood gold. Beginning in the mid-1940s, *la maggiorata*, or the physically well-endowed young woman, provided Italian moviegoers with an antidote to the destitution that pervaded the war and reconstruction years; a female possessing physical amplitude came to represent the strength and vitality of the nation. Two principal factors contributed to the reign of *la maggiorata* in the postwar Italian cinema: the boom in beauty contests and the emergence of Rome's film studios as "Hollywood on the Tiber." While hundreds, if not thousands, of people in Rome and the surrounding area eked out a living as extras at Cinecittà, the beauty contests provided a gateway for provincial and unknown young women to literally become movie stars, as in a fairy tale. The criteria for success had nothing to do with birth, education, or professional sponsorship.

The desirability of the voluptuous look represented a change from the prewar era on both sides of the Atlantic, when Mae West was one of the very few full-figured, overtly sexual stars in a Hollywood of slender sylphs and presexual pixies. The 1950s, on the other hand, witnessed the cinematic success of Brigitte Bardot, Anita Ekberg, Marilyn Monroe, and certainly, Sophia Loren. Early on, however, Loren stood out. Where her counterparts were passive sexual objects of masculine desire, Sophia, that force of nature, often brought something more participatory to the mix, even if only a wry, expressive glance.

PAGE 52: Ready to take on Hollywood, Sophia Loren gives the camera a seductive look during a break in the filming of *The Pride and the Passion* (1956). OPPOSITE: In the early 1950s, Loren posed for a hyperbolic number of playful pinups, considering them all dues toward her acting career.

*A*s a young teenager, Sofia Scicolone got her start in the beauty contests. Although she began adolescence as a shy, scrawny girl, who was not attractive by any standard criteria, she blossomed into a stunning teenager with a captivating figure. In 1974, Romilda Villani recalled to *Ladies' Home Journal*, "At thirteen—like a miracle from God, who wants to help you—she began to bloom slowly and naturally, like a flower, and become beautiful."

Sofia had been doing well in school, but times were hard, Romilda and Sofia were ambitious, and academics were a luxury. Shortly before turning fifteen, Sofia entered the Queen of the Sea beauty contest at the posh Press Club overlooking the Bay of Naples. She modeled an evening gown made by her grandmother Luisa out of the pink curtains from their apartment in Pozzuoli; her old, worn black shoes received two coats of whitewash. Sofia, chosen one of the Queen's twelve Princesses, received a prize that included a train ticket to Rome, 23,000 lire (about $35, a not-inconsiderable earning), several rolls of wallpaper, table linens, and some newspaper coverage. The prize made it possible for the Princess of the Sea and her mother to travel to Cinecittà to seek work as extras on the Hollywood epic *Quo Vadis?* (1950).

In the time between her extra work on *Quo Vadis?* and Ponti's discovery of her, Sofia made a living being photographed for photoplays called *fumetti* (now called *fotoromanzi*)—photographic stories laid out like comics with text in balloons. She gained some measure of public recognition through the extensive circulation of the *fumetti*, receiving hundreds of letters from admirers. Her sultry sensuality was evident enough to justify her being assigned the last name Lazzaro by an editor, a provocative reference to her ability to raise men from the dead.

The *fumetti* provided a decent living and an income more reliable than that of a beauty queen or sometime film actress. Posing for the *fumetti*, Sofia drew on the brief and far from naturalistic theatrical training she had received in Naples, adopting the broad conventional gestures and expressions deemed characteristic of the femme fatale. B-movie romances of the time bore narrative and stylistic similarity to the *fumetti*, and Sofia brought her clippings with her as she sought film work. Consequently, she obtained roles in such forgotten pictures as *Hearts at Sea* (1950) and *Bluebeard's Seven Wives* (1950).

Sofia Lazzaro also paid the rent in the early 1950s by doing what could be referred to as pinup duty, a stage that Marilyn Monroe also experienced. Loren has acknowledged feeling a connection to Monroe, and Tony Crawley, in *The Films of Sophia Loren*, very aptly describes Loren as "embodying all Italy's strengths as Marilyn Monroe conjured America's weaknesses." Tragically, Monroe was unable to find the median between her brains and her breasts; Sophia states in her autobiography: "[Monroe] didn't seem to get joy from her work, or much joy from anything else. If, at seventeen, she had found a father, as I found Carlo, I think that would have been her salvation." While the Actors'

Studio and Lee Strasberg were Monroe's safe harbor for a time, they were in no way equivalent to Loren's synergistic and serendipitous De Sica/Mastroianni/Ponti collaborations. Monroe's fate may have also been due, at least in part, to cultural differences between what makes cinema successful in Italy versus the United States.

Sofia Lazzaro's prolific work as a pinup girl in the mid-1950s has ensured an almost inexhaustible supply of photographs, running the gamut from saucy and suggestive to simply sweet and very staged. These images track her acquisition of her craft as a photographer's subject while also tracing visual experiments with makeup, hair color (including blonde), poses, and attire. Her practice with starlet attributes may well have acted as her college of modeling for media; it certainly introduces us to the nascent style of Sophia Loren.

The first photographs were made for immediate profit, but in late 1951, when Ponti began to manage her career, he used them to publicize Loren, creating recognition for her throughout Europe. So prolifically were postcards and other ephemera of her published throughout the 1950s in Germany, the Netherlands, Spain, Great Britain, and Sweden, as well as in Italy, that many survive today. Some show Sofia in film costumes, but many do not; most have the name "Sophia Loren" on the face.

*P*hotography plays a prominent role in *Tempi nostri* (*The Anatomy of Love*, 1953). A purely slapstick episode called "La macchina fotografica" pairs Loren with the film comedian Totò. The hugely popular Totò plays a lecher who purchases a camera for the express purpose of beguiling a comely young girl (Loren) to pose for him. In this traditional sex comedy, Sophia is merely the straight woman, the comic occasion of Totò's trademark burlesque take on lust.

A comic yet revealing account of a Roman photographer's model informs *La fortuna di essere donna* (*Lucky to Be a Woman*, 1955), an early Loren diva project, in which Sophia plays a Roman beauty named Antoinette, a stocking salesgirl. Adjusting her own stocking on the Appian Way, she is captured on film by Corrado, a paparazzo (played by Marcello Mastroianni), as he zooms by in an open car. Antoinette is a shapely blonde in a pastel sweater with a choker, a narrow, movement-impeding skirt, and pumps. When her picture is emblazoned on the cover of a tabloid paper, Antoinette reacts instantly: "You are going to manage me," she tells Corrado. "I'm going to be a model!" Corrado introduces her to Count Gregorio Sinetti (Charles Boyer), Rome's biggest screen-talent scout, enthusing, "There's a girl of character and temperament—not to mention what goes without saying!"

Over the course of the film, Antoinette goes from being a sexy sweater girl to a chic and elegantly mannered diva, but her real prize is a happy ending with the scrappy Corrado. Unlike American films of the period—such as Jean Negulesco's *How to Marry a Millionaire* (1953), in which the female dream is to achieve idleness—the working-class Antoinette wants and gets the job, not to mention the guy.

Loren also plays comedic sirens in *Peccato che sia una canaglia* (*Too Bad She's Bad*, 1954) and *Il segno di Venere* (*The Sign of Venus*, 1955). As in *La fortuna di essere donna*, the fashion in these films is modern urban sweater girl with form-fitting stretch dress from head to toe. The sausage-casing wardrobe Sophia sports in these comedies, combined with teetering high heels, produces her swingy walk and, by extension, her broad, seductive gestures. These outfits are peripherally interesting from an economic perspective, as Italy was then reestablishing its thriving knitwear-manufacturing industry.

OPPOSITE: *Inspired by the Roman ruins, Loren's character in* La fortuna di essere donna *obligingly reveals her own classical proportions, posing statuelike with her drapery rearranged. Charles Boyer, as the probably spurious Count Gregorio, directs her photo session enthusiastically.*

The best of her romantic comedies is *Peccato che sia una canaglia*, in which Mastroianni plays a dumb taxi driver who finds Loren and her family of thieves running circles around him. She does little more than plant her hands on her hips, sway a bit, roll her eyes at his naïveté, and focus on something outside the frame, as if to emphasize his limited view. But that's all she needs to do. Vittorio De Sica, who later directed both actors in *Matrimonio all'italiana* (*Marriage, Italian-Style*, 1964), seems to be giving the young leads comedic charm lessons in his role as Loren's larcenous father. The film was the masterful Neapolitan trio's first endeavor together, although their efforts over the following twenty years would often be with De Sica as director.

It is worth briefly revisiting the "wet look" subgenre here to mention that there was a lot of pinup appeal in those films. The babe in the bathing suit could be photographed on set for promotional purposes, with the image being sold for trading cards and a plethora of other possible reproductions. Between 1951 and 1955, Loren unloosed and sustained a cheesecake juggernaut. She was universally popular among photographers because of her willingness to take direction and then be creative and saucy—and hence highly marketable.

Although Loren certainly looks monumental in a bathing suit, it is interesting to note that by 1955, when her journeyman period had ended, she no longer sought to pose for such pictures as an end in itself. Most of her pinups after that date are editorial spreads for magazines, with accompanying information about her, paparazzi shots with her decided collusion, and film production stills. This change was, perhaps, an attempt on the part of Ponti and Loren to signal to the film industry that Sophia Loren had graduated from starlet.

While Sophia took on a number of sexy comedic roles, the darker side of the siren is also much in evidence in her career. That sense of disrepute and danger is captured in the wardrobes of some of those films. The successful costume pictures that Cinecittà turned out en masse in the early and mid-1950s featured clinging and draped "historical" wardrobes, as well as more than occasional flashes of skin. It was a natural progression from the sultry femmes fatales that Loren had depicted in the *fumetti* to the foreign and/or barbarian queens of her earliest starring vehicles, particularly *Aïda* (1953) and *Attila, flagello di Dio* (*Attila*, 1953). *Due notti con Cleopatra* (*Two Nights with Cleopatra*, 1953) proves once again, however, that it is in her comedies that Sophia's brand of sexiness finds its fullest expression.

According to Stella Bruzzi in *Undressing Cinema*, the classic attributes of screen sirens include self-conscious, exaggerated femininity; extreme artificiality; frequent wardrobe changes (unmotivated by action); and the use of distinctive, often anachronistic garments or accessories. All these are present in *Due notti con Cleopatra*, in which Cleopatra and the blonde slave Nisca are look-alikes but complete opposites in terms of temperament. Both are

OPPOSITE: Acting opposite Marcello Mastroianni in *Peccato che sia una canaglia*, Sophia vamps it up, posing like an amphibian sunning on a rock.

portrayed by Sophia Loren, who sports some of the most cartoonlike costumes in the history of cinema. But the tone that these costumes set is appropriate for the film, a broad farce that features an over-the-top performance by Alberto Sordi as a bumpkin in the palace guard. Rather than the typical sword-and-sandal film of the period, *Due notti con Cleopatra* is, in fact, a send-up of the genre.

The year is 31 B.C., and Cleopatra wears a succession of femme fatale fashions, beginning with a sheer chiffon negligee featuring gilt stripes and a geometric black collar, her black hair arranged in pointed bangs. She exchanges this outfit for a blue-gray, polka-dot column dress boasting satin swag shoulders and a bustle, plus a red shawl and a crowned turban. She then dons an ivory, vertical-striped, form-hugging satin sheath, enhanced with a metallic shrug and dangling earrings. Finally, she sports a white draped gown and a purple chiffon fanny wrap. She is all about cinema vamp, a barracuda of a woman who purchases poisons like perfume and eliminates her lovers in turn like insects. The still-teenage Sophia Loren is both comic-book siren and ingenue, not yet at ease in her costumes, but clearly displaying an innate sense of her physical appeal as she maneuvers her splendid body among her colleagues. As Nisca, the demure, blonde slave girl, Loren is adorned in a modest, draped, blue jersey gown with subtle geometric borders. To further differentiate queen and slave, Nisca has no costume changes. The members of the Egyptian queen's retinue are all outfitted in fifties-silhouette, geometric-patterned white gowns; a slapstick profusion of stripes is the only unifying theme among the costumes, though their graphic simplicity owes much to the *fumetti*.

Hollywood liked costume films, too, and the look of these films suited Loren and her fellow buxom actresses; after all, the first half of the twentieth century represented merely a hiatus in the preeminence of the hourglass shape as a feminine ideal. The most popular type of Hollywood costume film was, of course, the western. *Heller in Pink Tights* (1959) is an odd version of the breed. The film was directed by George Cukor, best known for "women's" films, whether slick and urbane contemporary comedies such as *Adam's Rib* (1949) or gripping melodramas such as *Gaslight* (1943). Cukor asked a friend, fashion photographer and artist George Hoyningen-Huene, to oversee the visual details of the picture. Hoyningen-Huene possessed a broad interpretation of "visual details," involving himself in everything from locations and the film in the camera to the wardrobe (overseen by the legendary Edith Head), hair, and make-up. As a result of Hoyningen-Huene's participation, the overall effect is much more Henri de Toulouse-Lautrec than Louis L'Amour. The vamp, Angela Rossini (Loren), is a comical actress-seductress who changes costumes dozens of times in the picture; she is, in effect, a nineteenth-century frontier Sophia Loren, carefully crafting her persona through feminine accoutrements and strategies to achieve fame in a career that is meaningful to her. As a western, the

O PPOSITE: Alberto Sordi adores the blonde slave Nisca in the comedy *Due notti con Cleopatra*. While Loren has also made earnest historical epics, this goofy sword-and-sandal parody is a panorama of absurd hairstyles and costumes.

film failed to find its audience, but as visual entertainment, it is exceptional, thanks to the Victorian costumes and the careful attention devoted to production details.

The pink tights referred to in the title deserve mention because they represent an earlier convention of the sex symbol. Nineteenth-century dramas sometimes afforded opportunities for actresses to appear in some form of implied nudity, usually a flesh-pink body stocking. This costume aroused exceptional acclaim for various actresses of that period, including Ada Mencken, to whom Loren's character refers by starring in *Mazeppa*. In this play within the movie, Loren, strapped to an actual horse, rides through the theater in a pink body stocking, accented by a bit of drapery that covers one breast. Such plays drew crowds, naturally, and created superstar followings for the actresses.

*O*ne of the reasons Sophia has done so many comedies may lie in her impressive sexual presence, the effect of which on her male costars is a staple of war-between-the-sexes humor. William Holden, who costarred with her in *The Key* (1957), said, uneasily, "I never saw so much woman coming at me in my entire life." In 1962, *Time* magazine stated that in Loren's Hollywood pictures, "she was matched with leading men whom she could have swallowed with half a glass of water."

At least one of Sophia's costars understood that the value of her sex appeal went far beyond the merely visual and amounted to money in the bank: after Loren gave John Wayne an inspired first screen kiss in *Legend of the Lost* (1957), Wayne, who was also the film's producer, chortled "Oh, you gorgeous investment."

With her towering figure and strong sexuality, Loren did seem to require a monumental leading man to take the authoritative role; John Wayne was one such actor, while Cary Grant—with whom rumor paired her in an intense flirtation—was another. Interestingly, however, her definitive film partnership did not place her opposite this type of male lead.

Marcello Mastroianni and Sophia Loren made a dozen films together, which put them neck and neck with Spencer Tracy and Katharine Hepburn as postwar film's most enduring couple. Mastroianni's suave image of bewildered, unexamined alienation is a perfect foil for Loren's vitality and feminine overdrive. About their partnership, Mastroianni remarked, "She acts, while I react," assigning the passive role to himself, willingly, knowingly.

The set pieces that most beautifully represent this statement are, naturally, the twin stripteases that Loren performs for Mastroianni in the films *Ieri, oggi e domani* (*Yesterday, Today and Tomorrow*, 1962) and *Prêt-à-Porter* (*Ready to Wear*, 1994). In the former, act she does, liltingly removing her clothes and swaying seemingly to some light jazz in the background, while Marcello reacts by crouching in a fetal position in the corner of the bed. The interplay between the two is so powerful that the image was selected for the movie poster.

OPPOSITE: Renowned Hollywood costumer Edith Head fits Loren for her role as Angela Rossini, a traveling player of 1880, in *Heller in Pink Tights*. Because of their period "S curve," the costumes demanded an unusual posture of the actress.

There is a longtime association between the sexy image of Sophia Loren and what the European fashion industry calls intimo, or lingerie. Many of her most memorable images feature her in articles intended as tools for seduction. It is in her Italian films especially that the role of lingerie is so prominent—and so artfully employed.

The ingenious costume designers who worked with Loren during the 1950s and 1960s were instrumental in perpetuating the image of Loren as sex goddess. Piero Tosi and Marcel Escoffier, in particular, crafted sensational undergarment designs for a number of her films.

Tosi was responsible for the black merry widow that Loren wore to great comic effect in *Boccaccio '70* (1961) and for the sexy lingerie in the famous striptease of *Ieri, oggi e domani* (*Yesterday, Today and Tomorrow*, 1962). In the former film, Loren, wearing a red structured bodice over a beautiful sheer black merry widow, causes the very emblem of masculine power, a bull, to turn tail. In the latter film, an exclusive Roman call girl named Mara wears a naughty combination of black lace bra, corselet, panties, and garter belt—with a brief little peignoir for terrace wear. Her accessories include bangle bracelets and an ankle chain. Recently, an Italian magazine cited Mara's as the century's most influential brassiere, freeing women to be comfortable and to breathe after centuries of constriction.

Tosi also created the tantalizing number that Sophia wears in *Matrimonio all'italiana* (*Marriage, Italian-Style*, 1964). Pictures of Sophia in this risqué outfit, as captured on set by photographer Tazio Secchiaroli, have been published widely, along with the actual film stills. An Alfred Eisenstaedt photograph of her in the outfit appeared on a cover of *Life* magazine.

The gown's vertical ribbon stripes and sparkly sequins were a tribute to Sophia's Amazonian stature, and reflected the stylized, sexual charge associated with working girls' working clothes. Likewise, Tosi's very transparent negligee featured spiders embroidered over the breasts, a subtly comic iconographic visual element. Like a spider—and like the conventional view of the prostitute as mantrap—Filumena is trying to capture Domenico (Mastroianni) in her web; the film's humanity lies in the twist that it is her profound concern for her children that drives her scheming, as well as her own genuine love for their father.

OPPOSITE: The phenomenal Filumena Marturano of *Matrimonio all'italiana*. In her best siren films, Loren is elaborately feminine and larger-than-life.

Escoffier created historically accurate equivalents of what is today called lingerie for Loren's characters in *Madame Sans-Gêne* (*Madame*, 1961), *Lady L* (1965), and *The Voyage* (1973). These undergarments are more white batiste and eyelet than black lace, but their effectiveness in showcasing Loren's appealing physique is much the same. In a corset, the actress's natural hourglass shape is enhanced and in turn enhances her vivaciously magnetic historical characters, without any of the dust or fading. In one of Loren's latest pictures, *Francesca e Nunziata* (2000), directed by Lina Wertmüller, Sophia is again resplendent in the embroidered lace and linen of the early twentieth century. The owner of a successful macaroni-manufacturing company, she can afford such labor-intensive handmade articles.

Intimo also expresses the interiority of the clothing worn beneath: in Roman Catholic Italy, the expressiveness of lingerie is a significant, even subversive message of sensuality, an open acknowledgment of human passions and frailty. Sophia Loren, in the lingerie of characters prim and profane, has brought that hidden message of sensuality to the world's screens.

For this riveting performance, which occurs in the episode "Mara of Rome," De Sica had her instructed by a real exotic dancer, and yet Loren, playing a hooker with a heart of gold, seems distant from that world, as wholesome as a lamb in her black merry widow and garters. She is playfully sheepish, and it is no tawdry performance that she delivers for Mastroianni. In fact, she never completely undresses, keeping the oath that she has made to God to take a weeklong hiatus from her profession. The second time around, thirty years later, in *Prêt-à-Porter*, Sophia is mature and magnificent. Yet this time, too, her divestiture fails to reach its expected climax—because Marcello, thirty years older, falls asleep.

The two Italian actors' most famous pairing, *Matrimonio all'italiana*, is a sunny farce in which Loren—as the longtime mistress of Mastroianni's wealthy Neapolitan character—schemes to get him to marry her. Impelled by the desire to help her sons—*their* sons—start out in life, her character gradually dominates his onscreen, echoing their dynamic in *Ieri, oggi e domani*. First seen as a doe-eyed, shorn-headed gamine hiding in a wardrobe, she gradually increases in splendor and actual stature throughout the film even as she ages, becoming middle-aged, slightly thick-waisted, and weary. The effect is accomplished through costume, makeup, hair—and acting. And it is this Filumena who, on a bleak hillside overlooking Naples, makes love with her man.

The 1960s sex-symbol Sophia is clearly a protofeminist, although her resulting dominance is as a wife and mother. Her power does not translate to control over anything in the patriarchal world.

It is clear that throughout her career Loren has pondered her image as a sex symbol. In her autobiography, she addresses the ambiguity that makes her such a potent sexual figure:

> *I think the quality of sexiness comes from within. People have always considered me a sex symbol, but in playing those roles that conveyed that impression, I never once deliberately said to myself, "Now, Sophia, play this real sexy, really set them on fire." I could not tell you what I did that made a particular role sexy; I simply played the character as I imagined her to be.*

In the end, it may be a statement Loren made at a press conference for *I girasoli* (*Sunflower*, 1969) at New York City's Radio City Music Hall that best describes the intelligent self-awareness that has made her a star unlike any other: "People think I have a hundred percent sex appeal, but it is only imagination. Maybe fifty percent is what I've got. The other fifty percent is their fantasies working on it."

O P P O S I T E : The sensational striptease in *Ieri, oggi e domani* shows no sign of sliding into obscurity. The combination of eroticism and slapstick required for the scene represented a serious professional challenge for the actress.

Chapter Four

Diva

*A*s much as any diva of Italian grand opera, Sophia Loren has a style that is larger than life. Elegant in the perfection of haute couture, impeccably made-up, and meticulously accessorized, she is the personification of glamour—both in public appearances and in her high-style films.

Dress designers and stars have long enjoyed a unique and intimate symbiosis. A star may receive special treatment in exchange for wearing a house's designs at high-profile events and identifying the outfits' creators; today it is understood that stars can choose from a smorgasbord of looks presented to them by a fashion house. The only variables in the practice revolve around how highly regarded the designer is and whether money will change hands. A new young starlet's natural equivalent is a new young designer, but a power diva like Sophia Loren is the equal of the House of Dior, Valentino, or Giorgio Armani. The Olympians of film can enjoy the discreet confirmation of status that comes from custom-made and one-of-a-kind designs—at least until the knockoffs go into production.

In her couture films, Sophia's carriage and acting ability enhance everything she wears, while her offscreen associations with the great fashion houses have brought glory to both the designers and their knowledgeable model. In recent years, Loren's long tenure as one of the world's most fascinating women and her enduring connection with her native land have made her a natural spokeswoman for the Italian fashion industry, rendering her a sort of stateswoman of chic.

Retrospectively, a childhood classmate of Loren reflected that the actress had an innate sense of her clothing style at a very young age. Loren biographer Warren G. Harris quotes Roseta D'Isanto, one of Loren's *compagne di banco* (literally "desk-mates") from public school: "She demonstrated and we all copied. No matter what she wore she always made it seem as if it had come from a boutique. She always wore very full skirts and tight blouses."

The serenely ambitious Loren understood early on the importance of glamour to her endeavor to become a movie star. As timing would have it, all areas of Italian design were booming. Ava Gardner and other American stars were turning to Italian designers such as Fontana Sorelle (Fontana Sisters) for chic, and Sophia knew she could do no less; she needed a war chest of magnificent fashions to compete with her contemporaries.

PAGE 70: Ella Bei, from the fashion house Knize, created the ornate costumes that Loren wears as Princess Olympia in *A Breath of Scandal* (1959), a romance set in pre–World War I Europe. OPPOSITE: Red velvet and ermine grace the luxuriant beauty in 1957, with some of her renowned jewels adding opulent accents.

Loren's 1957 move to Hollywood presented a complex fashion opportunity. Emilio Schuberth was one of Italy's grandest couturiers; in addition, he was wise in the ways of screen divas and recognized the mutual publicity benefits that stemmed from arrangements with them. Loren, who approached the designer in anticipation of her maiden voyage to Hollywood, was fortunate to work with him at such an early stage of her ascent. Schuberth's classical, stylized opulence, often manifested in contemporary designs cut of nostalgic renditions of classical fabrics, was the very thing for spinning a fantasy and bringing a touch of class to the Hollywood enterprise. Although over her five years as a cinema actress she had purchased an ample wardrobe and was a client of Monsieur Dior himself, Schuberth prepared a variety of sketches for Loren's review, and she selected forty-two outfits for her Hollywood "trousseau." In this, as in little else, she was on her own: Ponti, by his own admission, has a "tin ear" for couture.

Schuberth was the perfect introduction to couture for Loren in the guise of starlet, for he specialized in body-molded evening wear, and Sophia's hourglass shape was his ideal canvas. The son of an Austrian ladies'-glove maker and an elegant Neapolitan mother, Schuberth found that his fashion heritage prepared him well for the rigors of Hollywood on the Tiber. At his couture house on via Venti Settembre in Rome, he designed for some of the world's most celebrated and elegant women, including Brigitte Bardot, the American singer Abbe Lane, Sophia's "rival" Gina Lollobrigida, and the duchess of Windsor.

The wardrobe he designed for Loren's Hollywood debut included a variety of accessories—hats, gloves, furs, stoles, and filmy, transparent scarves—as well as lavish undergarments and peignoirs; all were as sumptuous as the magnificent gala gowns and cocktail and dinner dresses, which were, for the most part, strapless numbers accessorized with scarves that tied in the back. It was unusual for a couturier of Schuberth's standing to design intimate apparel, but it was fortuitous that he did so, since promotional stuntman Mario Natale worked hard to keep Loren's lingerie in the public eye. The palette of her wardrobe was overwhelmingly light, including pink, white, turquoise, champagne, and chartreuse; even though black is her favorite color, Loren included only five dresses in this hue, perhaps calculating that she would attract more attention at a formal occasion if she didn't wear the same color as all of the men.

Loren knew the Italian designers well, including Fontana Sorelle (Zoe, Micol, and Giovanna Fontana), whose atelier was the most popular fashion stop for Hollywood stars working in Rome. Fontana Sorelle designed Loren's wardrobe for *La fortuna di essere donna* (*Lucky to Be a Woman*, 1955), while Micol Fontana also appeared in the film, playing a couturiere called La Fontanesi. In the film, Antoinette (Loren) has a tortured relationship with dress and success, very much like Audrey Hepburn in director Billy Wilder's *Sabrina* (1954). Donning a bold print dress, would-be model and

Hemmets
Veckotidning

Nº 3
17 jan.

SOPHIA LOREN

JAN

55 ÖRE

Prinsessan Birgitta 21 år

Strålande bilder
trevlig artikel

movie star Antoinette goes resolutely to La Fontanesi, the silver-haired proprietress of a Roman couture salon, who sneers that if Antoinette wants to be taken seriously as a model, she will need to lose eight to ten pounds (3.5 to 4.5kg) and *never* wear print dresses, only black. The next scene finds Antoinette at home, fasting and dyeing her entire wardrobe black while periodically running to the grocer to check her progress on his meat scale.

There is more than a little biographical relevance in the transformation that Loren's character undergoes at the hands of her Pygmalion, the sinister "Count" Gregorio (Charles Boyer). When she tells him, "I want dresses that will knock everyone's eyes out!" he furnishes her with a succession of high-style ensembles, including a white redingote with velvet spread collar and accompanying gloves, hat, and veil; a modern and smart woven suit with architectural skirt pleat; and a white hat and black suit featuring big jewelry—all borrowed from La Fontanesi.

As Jean Negulesco later pointed out in reference to the filming of *Boy on a Dolphin* (1956), Loren preferred going barefoot. The next best thing was to have her footwear custom-made by Salvatore Ferragamo, who had originally founded his concern in Hollywood and subsequently returned to Italy, where he specialized in shoeing the greatest divas of the time, from Marilyn Monroe to Audrey Hepburn. Ferragamo was the only shoemaker to be credited in Sophia's films until the late 1960s, when Loren discovered the footwear designer Mario Valentino, a fellow Neapolitan, who also designed for celebrities such as Jacqueline Onassis and Ava Gardner.

*S*ophia's relationships with experts in the fields of fashion and beauty are critical to her successful maintenance of her diva image. The dress she wore to present at the 1999 Academy Awards, which was on display in the 2000–2001 Giorgio Armani retrospective at New York's Solomon R. Guggenheim Museum, represents her relationship with the latest designer in a series of fruitful collaborations.

The longest such alliance, though not exclusive, lasted almost three decades. Loren had been a client of Christian Dior remarkably early in her career: she was little more than a starlet when she became a client of Europe's premier couturier. When Monsieur Dior retired in 1955, Loren patronized his design successor, Yves Saint Laurent; then, beginning in 1961, she turned to Marc Bohan when Bohan was named to succeed Saint Laurent. Bohan, a seasoned couturier from Dior's London branch, inherited a distinguished clientele, an international who's-who peppered with film stars, including Loren. In several ways, Bohan was to Sophia what Givenchy was to Audrey. Bohan's trademark style—streamlined, almost minimalist, yet impeccably structured—was well suited to Loren's sophisticated look of the 1960s, '70s, and '80s. As is the case with the creations of Armani, whose clothing Loren now wears, the internal structure and the inherent control that Bohan's designs afford also allow the wearer to displace the body from the clothes. The surgical cut and precision tailoring that are characteristic of the great couture houses result in forms that are so personalized that they invest the well-dressed with a sense of ease and innate comfort. By turning to couturiers, Loren is assured of soft dressmaking, hand-finishing, and the finest fabrics available. The responsiveness to comfort and attention to detail that she champions in her book *Women & Beauty* are fundamental attributes of the great designers.

Bohan describes Loren as disciplined, modest, and astute, by which he means that she is detail-oriented and tireless in assuring that her clothing, like everything involving her profession, be managed with attention and accuracy. She certainly regards only what suits her as appropriate fashion; in general this has meant well-cut, precisely tailored clothing that emphasizes her waist, décolletage, and legs. She still adheres to this aesthetic, although her wardrobe today generally places decidedly less emphasis on her legs. No fashion victim, she collaborates with a designer to achieve the look she wants. She understands that part of the couturier–client relationship is up to her, but, appreciating the artistry and craft that go into couture, she also knows what should be left to the designer. She has a well-honed sense of the lines that favor her. For example, during the seasons of the sack dress and the chemise, Loren asked Bohan to create the fitted waists with full skirts that suit her body best.

At Loren's behest, Bohan also designed her wardrobe for her television specials of the 1960s as well as for several films of that decade and the 1970s, including *Arabesque* (1965), *A Countess from Hong Kong* (1966), *Le testament* (*Jury of One*, a.k.a. *The Verdict*, 1974), and *The Cassandra Crossing* (1976). When Loren was signed to star with Gregory Peck in *Arabesque*, producer-director Stanley Donen persuaded the studio to spend top dollar on really sensational fashions—he needed only cite the success of Givenchy's fashions on Audrey Hepburn for his 1963 film, *Charade*.

A great deal of time went into these special creations, and Donen required that all of the costumes be finished before shooting started. The twenty-five pairs of shoes and boots that the production called for, to be designed by Bohan's Dior colleague Roger Vivier, were equally opulent and labor-intensive and had to be ready in advance. Thus, before she even began memorizing her lines, Loren stopped in Paris for costume fittings with Bohan and Vivier. All told, the Dior bill for the film weighed in at about $125,000, the equivalent of roughly one-quarter of Sophia's superstar salary. As per her standard arrangement, Sophia took the clothes home at the end of the production; Monsieur Bohan suggests that most actresses do this, but without Loren's punctiliousness.

For the most part, the design styles for the films were inspired by the scripts as opposed to prevailing modes of dress. The guiding factors were character, action, and the amount of time the clothing would be onscreen—or at least

OPPOSITE: Yasmin, an oil magnate's mistress in *Arabesque*, wows a professor, played by Gregory Peck. Filmgoers were equally struck with her haute couture wardrobe by the House of Dior.

the length of time that it *should* have been onscreen. In the case of *Arabesque*, the Dior atelier found that there was almost an inverse relationship between complexity of construction and the duration of the costume's screen time.

The film's requirements were exceptional in many ways. Yasmin Azir (Loren), like the hieroglyphic that David Pollock (Gregory Peck) is trying to translate, is a cipher. Her looks pose an infinite variety of challenges to him and to the viewer. Is she with the good guys or the bad guys? We aren't supposed to know, so she repeatedly transforms herself from scene to scene, in transparent organdy and then in opaque vinyl, and always in highly stylish, impractical garb. She is an exotic bird in a gilded cage, a Middle Eastern mistress, and her world amounts to a runway collection of costly fashions. Everything is exaggerated: her negligee has a preposterous train—and her shoes! She wears not only bejeweled ones, but also thigh-high white boots! The palette is likewise ethereal, a panoply of golds and whites and Oriental reds—such stuff as dreams are made of, but not really good for running around in pursuit or for being pursued. In *Arabesque*, the fashions play the role that technological gadgets do in James Bond films; they're little fetishistic signposts alerting us to the fact that we are not in the realm of reality.

Bohan's white slip gown in *A Countess from Hong Kong* is a unique creation, having an exceptional relationship to both Loren's body and the character she portrays. This quality was requested by the director, Charlie Chaplin, as well as by Loren. Chaplin was very earnest and exacting about the countess's look, and Loren, awed by this iconic film figure, uncharacteristically deferred wholly to his authority. Alone among directors, Chaplin meticulously described the ways the dress would move, the ways it would be photographed, and the emotional pitch of the scenes in which it would appear. In fact, he went through the entire film with Bohan, carefully articulating the conceptual aspects of Loren's role and how she should look in each scene.

Countess Natascha Alexandroff (Loren) has a regal carriage and a silent, enigmatic way of insinuating herself into the life of a certain millionaire diplomat, Ogden (Marlon Brando), on a luxury liner returning to the United States from Hong Kong. Despite the fact that she is penniless and has been for some time, she has exquisite taste and knows how to economically illustrate her nobility in the minimalism of dress and gesture. Her slip dress, so demure and so revealing, is built architectonically, like the couture masterpiece it is. It is audaciously undecorative and deliberately shies away from being too openly seductive: the décolletage is restrained and the straps seem more utilitarian than provocative. All the details of the gown's construction are invisible. The dress could not succeed without Sophia's erect posture, as any laziness of waist or hip would immediately be broadcast in wrinkles; a coy imitator of a slip, it is actually a treacherous dress to wear. Dancing in this dress, Natascha enchants Ogden completely.

O PPOSITE: "Never has so much been poured into so little," Charlie Chaplin exclaimed when Loren first came on set in the Dior slip dress in which her countess from Hong Kong, Natascha, would so impress Marlon Brando's Ogden.

Everything Loren wears in the film, from gigantic pajamas to a Polynesian sarong, hugs her in exactly the reactive fabrics that will act as a counterpoint to her small, suppressed activities. She is very much a pantomime countess in the picture, and the burden of suggesting that a wiggly youthfulness and playfulness lie trapped beneath that worldly White Russian austerity is transferred to her clothing.

Marc Bohan also designed fashions for *Le testament*, in which Sophia plays opposite Jean Gabin. In the film, the almost forty-year-old Loren and the almost seventy-year-old Gabin are adversaries. She plays Teresa Lioni, an underworld widow from Lyons who resorts to kidnapping the wife of the chief magistrate (Gabin) in order to force him to free her son, whom she believes to be innocent of murder. The contrast between her role as someone involved in organized crime and her identity as a mother is expressed in her Dior wardrobe of stoic and luxe tailoring versus showy feminine sensuality. One dress that she wears—made of black chiffon with sheer sleeves, low décolletage, and a short hemline—is what Bohan considers to be her definitive look, best for her figure and body language. The tailored suits and the superior-quality double-faced wool coat that she wears do much to define her character's intractability and taste for finery, as well as her awareness of behaving duplicitously in tragic circumstances.

A designer must look beyond fashion, incorporating the client's personality and style, as well as how she inhabits her clothes. Bohan points out that Sophia Loren's style personifies this philosophy: when she is satisfactorily dressed, she feels secure, and that means that she is free to focus on the performance. "It has nothing to do with glamour," Bohan asserts. "Sophia Loren understands that perfectly." He cites as an example *The Cassandra Crossing*, a film that Loren very much wanted to do. Bohan's work on the film was not called for by anything in the script, but it was Loren's familiarity with his clothes that made her wear Dior for that film.

The outfits for the episode "Anna of Milan" in *Ieri, oggi e domani* (*Yesterday, Today and Tomorrow*, 1962) were designed by Marc Bohan for Christian Dior. Not only do they contribute to both plot and character, but they are right from that season's collection. In the film, Sophia wears a taupe turtleneck knit chemise dress with a leather belt, a fur-lined trench coat, and a fedora. The costumes are neither fantasy fashion, as in *Arabesque* and *Boccaccio '70* (1961), nor the usual flattering Loren styles, but they do express the "today" of the title eloquently. These are precisely the sort of looks that Monsieur Bohan stated Loren did not wear for herself, as they did nothing whatsoever for her. It is interesting to note that these unsympathetic fashions are worn by an unsympathetic character; Anna of Milan is a harsh cynic, created by a keen social observer, Alberto Moravia. The character looks affluent, yet, in contrast to the countess from Hong Kong, she lacks innate good style—she seems to demonstrate no sense of refinement or delicacy of instincts.

OPPOSITE: In the episode of *Ieri, oggi e domani* titled "Anna of Milan," Loren's character is a woman of means in a Dior shift; her accessories include a lover (Mastroianni) and a beloved automobile.

Loren remained a loyal client of Dior for decades and wore furs designed by Frédéric Castet, of the Dior fur salon, to important events. At the same time, in both her film and personal wardrobes, she wore designs of other Paris couture houses. The year 1960 was a stylish one for Loren: *A Breath of Scandal*, *It Started in Naples*, *Heller in Pink Tights*, and *The Millionairess* were all released that year. For the title role in *The Millionairess*, a screen adaptation of George Bernard Shaw's play, Loren wore an appropriately high-style couture wardrobe created by Pierre Balmain, one of the young Turks of Parisian postwar haute couture. After working at Lucien Lelong's atelier beside Dior before the war, Balmain founded his own couture establishment in 1945. His clientele, which included Katharine Hepburn, Marlene Dietrich, and Brigitte Bardot, appreciated the elegance and soft fluidity of his designs.

Not surprisingly, given his movie-star patrons, Balmain's house designed wardrobes for a number of films. His creations graced Danielle Darrieux, among others, in French films during the 1950s and began to appear in Hollywood films in the early 1960s. A young German designer who started at Balmain in 1957 began to assume responsibility over the work that the atelier was doing for films, including the modern designs of *The Millionairess*. His name was Karl Lagerfeld.

The Balmain wardrobe for *The Millionairess* is unjustifiably less celebrated than the couture in *Arabesque*, perhaps because couture houses were much more elite in 1960, whereas they had become trendy by 1966. Loren appears almost tight-laced in a corset, as well as in head-to-toe leather—decidedly not 1960 runway fashions! Epifania Parerga (Loren), an absurd character created by George Bernard Shaw, is a regular fashion doll, dressing and, more often, undressing throughout the film, and giving us an intimate look at each of her outfits. The reported cost of the costumes was $75,000, a figure not so astonishing given the number of extravagant fashions and the opulence of the materials. The *pelle*, or calfskin, dress she wears is the absolute pinnacle of the leather worker's art, with a drape like silk. The silk negligee and daywear that she dons also boast the fine quality that the couture houses command.

Guy Laroche, among the French innovators in ready-to-wear, traveled to the United States in 1955 to study manufacturing methods. His couture house, which he opened in 1957, drew a young and chic clientele who favored Cristóbal Balenciaga's bold, clean cuts but wanted designs that were both more playful and more practical. Sophia Loren's portrayal of a Laroche vendeuse in *Five Miles to Midnight* (1961) was enhanced by a wardrobe typical of the young professional fashion workers in Paris at that time. The work uniforms had clean lines with a minimum of individual variations, and could easily be adapted for evening activities, such as dancing in smoky jazz clubs. There is something appropriately film noir about the utility, ease, and lack of detail that pervade Loren's wardrobe, especially the black plastic trench coat she wears in the terrifying climax of the film.

O P P O S I T E : The Dior furrier Frédéric Castet designed for La Loren for two decades.

For Lina Wertmüller's film *Fatto di sangue fra due uomini per causa di una vedova* (*Blood Feud*, 1978), Loren's fashions were made by the Norwegian designer Per Spook. A onetime apprentice under Marc Bohan at the House of Dior, Spook opened his own concern in Paris in 1977. He not only designed Sophia's costumes for the Wertmüller picture, but also provided filmy, clinging silk dresses for Loren's U.S. publicity tour promoting her Coty perfume, called Sophia, which debuted late in 1980. Coty did concerted market research before committing to the pioneering star-named perfume. Loren's image apparently met all of the company's requirements, and she was asked to both select the scent—she picked jasmine and rose—and market it. Her creative control extended to the choice of designs for the bottle and box. The campaign for the perfume's launch included a film festival and personal appearances throughout the United States and Canada, as well as television interviews. The Fragrance Foundation awarded the perfume its top honors in 1981, but its democratically priced line, which included powder and soap, was overshadowed eventually by subsequent star perfumes, such as Elizabeth Taylor's Passion, which targeted a much wealthier market.

The era in which *Fatto di sangue fra due uomini per causa di una vedova* is set, the 1920s, suggested the film's look, one that was well suited to Spook's designs; the proportions and materials suited the fanciful as well as the sensible Sophia. During the 1970s, Spook catered to customers who appreciated his witty and feminine prints and swingy short skirts, as well as those who traveled light—he pioneered fabrics that allow dresses to be packed into small bundles.

*I*n 1966, after completing *A Countess from Hong Kong*, Loren accepted an invitation to serve as president of the jury of the nineteenth annual Cannes Film Festival. The renowned festival is always a twenty-four-hours-a-day spectacle of glamour and fantasy, but for the occasion, Bohan designed a particularly spectacular white chiffon gown for her first evening fete as president. As the president, and as a woman amid the male jury, Loren was the focal point for the assembled audience and journalists. Bohan's radiant and ethereal fashions photographed beautifully in the variable light of the festival, which ranged from artificial at night to searing daylight. The gossamer, fairy-godmother, and flashbulb-reflecting taffeta and metallic fabrics of Sophia's Cannes repertoire accentuated her rich, warm complexion, her hair, and her elaborate jewelry. The presidential wardrobe eclipsed that of all starlets and grandes dames in attendance. Crowds formed at the entrance of the Palais du Festival to observe Madame President's astonishing changes of clothing.

A month earlier, without fanfare, Loren had bought an even more special dress at Christian Dior: her bridal outfit, a pale yellow silk dress and coat. For the discreet ceremony, she carried lilies of the valley, which happened to be Monsieur Dior's trademark flower, as the mayor of Sèvres married her to Carlo Ponti. Her second and definitive marriage

O P P O S I T E : Sophia interprets George Bernard Shaw's millionairess with an assist from the House of Balmain. As Epifania, Loren is teamed with a series of costumes that nearly steal the film.

to Ponti (the first, a Mexican wedding by proxy in 1957, turned out not to be legal), it was also a noteworthy occasion in her career because there was no press coverage. The Pontis kept the ceremony completely private—not even the Dior archives hold any images of the ensemble.

In *Sophia Loren: A Biography*, Warren G. Harris includes an insightful anecdote told by Elizabeth Taylor—another veteran Dior customer during Bohan's tenure—to one of her friends. In 1973, when Richard Burton was staying in the guest house of the Villa Ponti, awaiting the start of production on what would be De Sica's last film, *The Voyage* (1973), his oft-estranged mate flew to Rome to join him. Taylor later recounted the way in which Loren received her: "Madame Ponti was wearing a Dior suit, a Dior handbag, Dior shoes and Dior gloves. Can you imagine? She was standing at the front door of her own house, waiting to greet me, in *gloves*!"

If Sophia Loren appeared enamored of fashion during the 1960s—the decade that had begun with her triumph as a ragged survivor in *La ciociara* (*Two Women*, 1960)—fashion happily requited her affection. The visionary Diana Vreeland, then editor in chief of *Vogue*, featured Sophia on a number of the magazine's more striking and memorable covers; in 1970, Loren graced the front of the all-important December *Vogue*. This was particularly significant, since Vreeland conferred special status upon the December issues; she thought of them as special gifts to her readers, and so these displayed the most provocative photography and design of any magazine of the time. This was the last December issue to be produced under Vreeland's aegis. *Vogue* in that period was something like film: a complex, creative endeavor that gathered a collaborative and changing cast of the most gifted and imaginative artists in order to sell otherworldliness and beauty to an audience of avid escapists. Both the graphic design of the magazine itself and the clothing (or, sometimes, lack thereof) depicted in its editorial pages were departures from any known reality. What Vreeland and her cohorts were manufacturing was an avant-garde presentation of style that was bold and dynamic. Loren, at this point in her mid-thirties and long an established goddess herself, was photographed by the Olympians of fashion photographers, divinities such as Irving Penn, Milton Greene, Richard Avedon, and Neal Barr. In 1980 she was recruited for the famous Blackglama ad campaign "What Becomes a Legend Most?" For this, she was photographed by the great Bill King.

In the late 1980s Loren began to patronize Italian designers again, particularly Valentino. Valentino Garavani started his business on the via Condotti in Rome in 1959 and managed to be included in a key slot in the Italian fashion collections in Florence shortly thereafter. He made his reputation as the couturier of the international jet set, including such luminaries of chic as Jacqueline Kennedy, Princess Margaret, Jane Fonda, Farah Diba, and Elizabeth

OPPOSITE: Creating an eccentric intersection of images, Secchiaroli photographed Loren as seen, quite literally, through Richard Avedon's eyes. This shoot represents only one of Loren's remarkable collaborations with the great photographers.

Taylor. Like Sophia, Valentino favors crimson as his signature color and knows how to wield it with ever-fresh vigor. It was a crimson Valentino suit that Loren sported in her mobile duties as grand marshal of New York's Columbus Day parade in 1984. Valentino's connection to the heart of Rome, with his current atelier by the Spanish Steps, no doubt exerts a force on those nostalgic for the glamour of Cinecittà and the Italian style that frames it.

Loren, who had avoided the publicity of the collections in her early couture days, was a high-profile front-row spectator at Valentino's shows beginning in 1984, when she left her home in Paris to appear, resplendent in Valentino sequins, at his spring/summer couture collection in Rome. So devoted was Loren to the Italian designer that when the House of Dior held a lavish fortieth-anniversary party in Paris in 1987, she wore an opulent Valentino gown to the event! Despite her gown's label, she was seated at the same table as the first lady of France, Claude Pompidou, and Bernard Arnault, Dior's new owner. When Sophia accepted her honorary Oscar in 1991—receiving the only standing ovation of the evening—she again wore Valentino.

*F*ashion and films merge in a surreal, high-style crossover in Robert Altman's *Prêt-à-Porter* (*Ready to Wear*, 1994), which envelops Loren in the fashion universe of Paris. Some of the film's footage was shot during actual runway shows, while some of the scenes were simply staged versions. The media sent to cover the actual collections were magnetically drawn instead to the magnificent, sixty-year-old diva. With the crossover between reality and fantasy, Sophia was part of the zaniest season of runway collections ever. Outfitted in her Gianfranco Ferré for Dior creations and enormous Jean Barthet hats, surrounded by real press and SAG extras, Loren was asked to weigh in on various aspects of Paris fashion. *Women's Wear Daily*, following her through a day of mock fashion shows, queried Loren on how she had liked the collection. "I wasn't really thinking about the collection," she replied, "because they were filming me."

A few years before *Prêt-à-Porter*, Loren was photographed by Michael Comte in Ferré fashions for Italian *Vogue*. Ferré, a Milanese who had been an independent designer since 1978, succeeded Marc Bohan as artistic director of the House of Dior in 1989. Ferré's work has been recognizably informed by Italian cinematic influences, particularly the high-style films of Federico Fellini and Michelangelo Antonioni. He designs powerful clothes for women, clearly drawing upon his education as an architect; in fact, *Women's Wear Daily* has called him the Frank Lloyd Wright of Italian fashion. Ferré's appreciation of the Italian cult of film stars, particularly those of the golden age, extends to both Sophia Loren's biography and her present-day image. Born a decade after Loren, he is simultaneously inspired by her film career and contributing to its furtherance in a sublimely sophisticated synergy.

OPPOSITE: Friend and fashion legend Valentino Garavani sketched Loren's gown for the 1991 Academy Awards, at which Loren received an honorary Oscar.

Valentino
for Sophia Loren
91

PE91- M169FL
ACADEMY AW

*H*ats both protect a person and project a personality. Compositionally, they balance a face, particularly one with generous features. They can complete a self-consciously put-together appearance or add humor, character, or narrative to a spontaneous look.

It is no wonder that Sophia Loren is so taken with hats: she has a wonderful face for them. Her large eyes and mouth never threaten to be eclipsed by even the most extravagant head covering, and she has the imposing physical stature that allows her to don even the most oversize numbers without being swallowed up by them.

The Paris hat designer Jean Barthet was a lifelong friend of Loren. He designed her hats for decades, creating in particular many variations on the *casquette*, a hat with a visor and little or no brim that is based on a specific type of military helmet. Loren valued Barthet's artistry and skill as a couturier of hats, understanding that the labor and originality that went into each design qualified it as a beautiful and collectible work of art.

In a number of Loren's films, the hats she sports play a part in the story or help to define her character. In *Ieri, oggi e domani* (*Yesterday, Today and Tomorrow*, 1962), for instance, Loren's urbanite femme fatale, Anna of Milan, wears a hat to go incognito while trysting with a man from a lower social class. In an evocation of American film noir, she sports a taupe-colored fedora with a brim angled menacingly over the

brow. At the other end of the social spectrum, in *La bella mugnaia* (*The Miller's Beautiful Wife*, 1955), Sophia's floppy straw hat is meant to show how rustic a peasant she is. Blithe and appealing in her picture hat of summer straw, she is as enchanting as a shepherdess from a seventeenth-century pastoral scene. (Picture hats are so named because they are like those seen in eighteenth-century portraits of landed ladies by Thomas Gainsborough and others.)

Some of Loren's most memorable characterizations are enhanced by hats, as in *The Millionairess* (1960), where the delightful chapeaux echo the personality of the fanciful protagonist, Epifania, who is chic and slightly imbalanced. Both the scale and whimsy of her hats are pronounced. One is a sheer, wiggly garden-party picture hat, while another is an exaggerated little textured straw hat of the shape called *postillion*, named for the riders who once guided horse-drawn vehicles and wore such accessories. More recently, Loren bore magnificent millinery in *Prêt-à-Porter* (*Ready to Wear*, 1994). In this film, she amazed audiences with her

impossibly large, parody picture hats. So striking was she in these crowning glories that she was subsequently immortalized in one on a Somalian postage stamp!

OPPOSITE, TOP: A hat model extraordinaire, Sophia donned a fresh straw number with flowers for a magazine cover; the hat is a timeless reminder of head coverings of previous centuries and of her native southern Italy.

OPPOSITE, BOTTOM: A fedora in *Ieri, oggi e domani* is one of the modish hats that aided Loren in creating the character of Anna. The deep brim and perfectly balanced angle add mystery to Anna's gaze.

ABOVE: An expression of both haute couture fantasy and trademark Sophia Loren humor, the hat seen here is a sort of biomorphic black halo. *Prêt-à-Porter* made oversize hats a leitmotiv of her character, perhaps deliberately drawing upon Loren's history as a hat lover.

Christian Dior

GIANFRANCO FERRÉ

LEFT: This Gianfranco Ferré design for Loren in *Prêt-à-Porter* reinterpreted a gabardine suit from his first Dior collection that he says he "rendered 'dramatic' for her with a big bow 'à la Dior' and an enormous hat and veil."

RIGHT: The deeply dipping black chiffon gown that Gianfranco Ferré created for *Prêt-à-Porter* was an adaptation of a design from his first collection for Dior (fall/winter 1989–90). Ferré customized it for Loren with what he calls "a breathtakingly low-cut neckline and a tiny waist."

Christian Dior

GIANFRANCO FERRÉ

Of Loren, Monsieur Ferré says, "She is an adorable woman with a great sense of humor, overwhelming humanity, and charisma. A woman any designer would love dressing, also because she has a perfect grasp of what makes the most of her figure and thus is able to choose her clothes with great confidence." Ferré says that his designs for her reflected elegance in the Dior mode, reconciling set requirements, Sophia's personal style, and the traits of her character.

In *Prêt-à-Porter*, Loren, who has negotiated the role of fashion in her life for half a century, surely enjoyed the film's woolly and acerbic ironies. Ferré outdid himself: his precise and elegant fashions are perfect for Isabella de la Fontaine (Loren), the newly widowed spouse of the president of the French organization that oversees the national haute couture. The clothes are diva-sleek and overstated, with polka-dot bows and padded shoulders *extraordinaires*. The ultrachic Paris couture of sharply tailored and dramatically draped pinstripes and silks, as worn captivatingly by the preternaturally engaging sexagenarian, was the real star of the season.

An official dinner for Italian president Oscar Luigi Scalfaro in 1996 gave the White House an opportunity to honor a roster of eminent Italian-Americans, including Martin Scorsese, Nicolas Cage, Jon Bon Jovi, and Mario Cuomo. Seated next to then-president William Jefferson Clinton was the seemingly ageproof Sophia, in an architectural, low-cut white beaded dress by Armani. (The down-to-earth diva later confessed to starving, since she found her dinner companion so interesting that she neglected her meal in order to ask him questions.)

Sophia wore an electric blue Armani dress when, in her role as ambassador-at-large for the city of Rome to promote fashion in the Eternal City, she met with the media to present the high-fashion schedule for 1998. And the best fashion moment of the 1999 Oscar ceremony was unquestionably Sophia Loren's arrival onstage. Clad in black Armani, she confidently strode toward the audience and then presented the Oscar for best foreign language film to her countryman Roberto Benigni with a spontaneous hug.

She has professed surprise at the intense enthusiasm of the dress's reception, given its monastic simplicity in comparison to most of the other designs present. The world-famous décolletage was discreetly veiled in black chiffon that extended from a high neckline to the wrists. What the dress provided in the Loren tradition, however, was impact and an awareness of the movement happening inside it: the fabric had so much stretch that she could have performed aerobics in it, distinguishing it from 99 percent of all spectacular gowns at ceremonial occasions. In fact, when Loren opened the envelope and gleefully announced Benigni's name, she needed every bit of the dress's give to accommodate her great, warm, Italian gesture. At the same time, the dress draped her closely, allowing for her hourglass figure to make its enthralling promenade across the stage. Sophia Loren's look at the 1999 Oscars was the fortunate result of many years of research and development by both Armani and Loren.

In fact, the fashion name most likely to be associated with Sophia Loren in recent years is Giorgio Armani. His subdued yet stylish lines seem just right for a longtime icon who still stops traffic. In her tribute to the designer in the catalog for the Guggenheim Armani retrospective, Loren celebrates his nonsensational and peaceful reliability as the antithesis of today's fashion-world practices. Similarly, after the designer's spring/summer 2000 fashion show, she told *Women's Wear Daily*, "When you dress in Armani, you can be sure you'll never look like a Christmas tree."

Giorgio Armani was born in Piacenza, a small town near Milan, two months before Sophia Loren. His mother was his most profound influence, a style-conscious woman who was skilled with a needle and made clothing for her children. His family included a number of artisans, but Armani attended medical school in Milan and did his military service before changing course and becoming interested in fashion. He worked both at the Milan store of the Rinascente chain and at the tailoring house Cerruti before introducing his own designs at the Sala Bianca in 1970. His own name venture, founded in 1975, soon entered into an association with Fred Pressman of Barneys and was discovered by Hollywood. His early innovations were well-cut, unstructured men's jackets featuring a body-skimming drape hitherto unknown in menswear anywhere. Since 1980, he has been hailed in New York as the Michelangelo of fashion and widely credited with creating a niche for Italian fashion in New York.

The fashion industry has embraced Sophia Loren as the matriarch of diva glamour. Not only did she receive the Council of Fashion Designers of America Lifetime of Glamour Award in 1999, but she was named honorary president of the Rome Fashion Agency; in that capacity, she officiated regally over a televised fashion parade on Rome's Spanish Steps in 1999.

Sophia Loren, certainly the most philosophical of diva sex symbols, takes advantage of her new fashion role—and the public appearances that go along with it—to express her values. Troubled, for example, by the image of chic being represented by thin fashion models, she urges Armani and others to employ runway models with breasts and bottoms, and she herself frequently sports her oversize spectacles, even with evening wear.

Returning to Sophia's earliest styles, Dolce & Gabbana, together with Steven Meisel, continue to be inspired by Loren's films and the tone of 1950s Naples and Rome. In their advertising, they direct their models, such as Linda Evangelista and Isabella Rossellini—the latter the offspring of Cinecittà royalty—to imitate the gestural style and sexy naturalism of the classic black-and-white De Sica and Fellini films. These representatives of the young fashion establishment celebrate the world of Italian cinema and the paparazzi—the world that begat Sophia Loren and continues to reengage the creative art of fashion.

OPPOSITE: At the 71st Academy Awards in 1999, Oscar presenter Sophia Loren stole the show as much for her columnar black Armani and radiant good looks as for the enthusiastic bear hug she gave fellow-Italian Roberto Benigni.

Chapter Five

Icon

*A*s early as 1955, *Life* magazine called her Europe's number one cover girl, and she may still be one of the most photographed celebrities ever. The world media have been more than pleased to cooperate with her in her ascent from diva to icon. Clearly, however, Loren triumphs in more than mere quantity, just as she is far more than the fuel of a legendarily successful publicity and promotion machine. Few stars have been in the public eye as long, and perhaps none have exercised the scrupulous oversight of their own myth-building to the degree that Sophia has.

From the beginning, Carlo Ponti and Sophia Loren were sophisticated participants in the symbiotic relationship between stars and the press. And they became masters of the publicity stunt: in the 1950s and 1960s Loren learned the value of keeping her image in the public consciousness. Though it has been decades since the icon Loren has engaged in such antics, one of the most outrageous Ponti-Loren promotion ploys was one that deserves to go down in the annals of exploitation—even if it is not clear exactly who was being exploited. It somehow became known that La Loren was making a trip to Rome's via Condotti to purchase brassieres; the news caused such a mob of men to form that three fire brigades had to be summoned to retrieve the starlet, who was "trapped" in a changing room.

When Loren won her Academy Award for *La ciociara* (*Two Women*) in 1962, careful planning and a bit of a gamble paid off in one of the great publicity coups of the decade, garnering her (and her film) unprecedented worldwide attention—in absentia. Though she was nominated for an Oscar for her work in De Sica's soon-to-be-classic, Loren was in Rome with Ponti during the awards ceremony, with the uninamed Pierluigi, a paparazzo and friend of Tazio Secchiaroli, on hand. When at 6:30 A.M. Cary Grant telephoned with the news of her win for *La ciociara*, Ponti and Loren immediately called in the troops. Her whole family, De Sica, and the available press were all summoned to her apartment to record her jumping for joy in her man's silk robe and slippers.

Only a week earlier, *Time* magazine had speculated about what Sophia would wear for the Oscars; her subsequent change of mind resulted in a much more personal ceremony, one that has been remembered much longer than if she had carried out plan A.

PAGE 98: In 1971, Tazio Secchiaroli caught an ephemeral image of Loren in Spain during the filming of *Bianco, rosso, e…* (*The White Sister*). Here, Loren is a resplendent, vital whole, sparkling with all of her many facets. OPPOSITE: Image maintenance requires the right apparel. Here, Loren sports a white gala cape with shawl fringe, designed by Frédéric Castet for Dior.

Sophia Loren started on the cover of dime-store *fumetti* in 1952 and never looked back. There are countless magazine covers from throughout the world carrying her image, some heralding an in-depth profile of the actress and some simply hoping to boost circulation with the expressive, iconic actress up front.

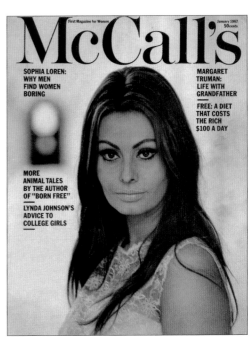

*L*oren's rise from beautiful and talented actress to international icon is due in part to the fact that she has been an invaluable asset in promoting both herself and the projects with which she is associated. Part of her success in this area lies in her gift for and knowledge about posing for photographers—a skill that perhaps comes from her long-ago training as a pinup girl. Sam Shaw, the definitive independent on-set photographer, chronicled Sophia Loren from 1956, when she was rehearsing for *The Pride and the Passion*, through the production of *Matrimonio all'italiana* (*Marriage, Italian-Style*) in 1964. Shaw's candids followed Loren home after her day's work, captured portraits of her mother and sister in Loren and Ponti's apartment in Rome, and showed Sophia and Carlo in her rented Beverly Hills home during her time in Hollywood (as an unmarried couple, they could not share digs). These widely reproduced images gave the public an intimate sense of the young actress's playful, uninhibited style, as well as of the fierce industry and discipline she has always dedicated to her craft. In Shaw's photographs Loren is rarely in repose; rather, she appears to be in perpetual motion, always moving swiftly across the frame like a comet.

Sophia must have learned a lot from her relationship with Shaw, because she sagely made Tazio Secchiaroli—the original paparazzo and the inspiration for Fellini's *La Dolce Vita* (1959)—her personal photographer when he left his initial profession. After years spent energetically invading the privacy of the rich and famous, especially the great and near-great of Cinecittà, and feeding the scandal sheets unauthorized images of them, Secchiaroli became a member of their inner circle, creating iconic images at their behest. Besides Loren, Secchiaroli lyrically documented the worlds of Mastroianni, Fellini, and Antonioni for the entirety of his freelance career, from 1962 to 1983.

As her still photographer, Secchiaroli chronicled Loren for almost twenty years, both on the set and at home; he was an interesting choice because his work would always retain from his paparazzo days a slightly gritty, stolen quality that connoted his model's authenticity and spontaneity beneath the glamour. Theirs was a collaboration, as Sophia created the perfect opportunity to shape her own celebrity. Indeed, Loren is among the few stars who studiously and assertively directs this aspect of her career. Her arrangement with Secchiaroli had an additional benefit: there are no extant photographs of the period showing Sophia Loren being hounded by the press.

She once told photographer Sam Shaw, "Posing for the camera is a love affair." But it is also serious business. At the hospital where she gave birth to her younger son, Edoardo—named for Edoardo De Filippo—Loren had herself rolled on a gurney into an operating theater for a press conference to introduce the new arrival. Secchiaroli was in awe of her professionalism, as he told journalist Alan Levy: "Sophia always wants to see every picture that's taken of her. She even checks every contact and every print of the stills that are made on the set or on location. . . . She was fed up

O P P O S I T E : What do you get when you cross the world's most lyrical photographer of women, Sam Shaw, with perhaps the most intuitive camera presence of any era? This sublime portrait of Sophia Loren.

with stagy stills that made her look like a statue posing." Nor was Secchiaroli the first to observe Loren's supervisory impulses. As Anatole Litvak, who directed her in *Five Miles to Midnight* (1961), remarked to *Time* magazine in 1962, "Nothing is too small to demand her attention if it has something to do with her career. For example, she keeps a magnifying glass beside her bed, where she goes over the tiny contact prints of her publicity pictures."

Not surprisingly, Loren also worked with the century's preeminent fashion photographers. Richard Avedon, Neal Barr, Bill King, Alfred Eisenstaedt, Lord Snowdon, and Irving Penn all covered Loren in a variety of editorial assignments, ranging from psychological explorations to hallucinatory abstractions. And each brought into public view a different perspective on the multifaceted gem that is Sophia. A glance at her magazine covers over time reveals as much creative reinvention on her part as any star of the century—including the legendarily protean Madonna.

As early as 1966, the breadth of images of Sophia Loren was vast. In that year, The Museum of Modern Art in New York mounted an exhibition of photographs of her that MoMA director René d'Harnoncourt declared to be the museum's first exhibition of an artist who was also a subject. The opening events were sponsored by MGM, the studio that was about to release her star vehicle *Lady L* (1965). La Loren was resplendent in haute couture white organdy with flowers and a showstopping necklace of diamonds with a large emerald. The exhibition, an insightful assemblage that highlighted Loren's uniquely active participation in her own career and celebrity, was a conjunction of two areas of popular culture: still photography and cinema. Evident throughout—in on-set candids, stills, and posed portraits—were the many levels of Loren's artistry. Her intelligent collaborations with great directors, writers, photographers, production and costume designers, and makeup artists and hairstylists were all on view at the Modern.

There is nothing superior about Loren's attitude toward stardom; she does not look down on her audiences, but rather brings them up to her pedestal for a look around. For fifty years she has never ceased to be appreciative of the good fortune she has enjoyed since turning fifteen. One of the qualities that connects her with her audience is that, in a sense, she shares their perspective about the glamorous existence she leads. This is one reason why the Villa Ponti has been photographed in tireless detail and why Loren hosted a television special from it; with true Italian hospitality, she invites her audience into her world. Like them, she is awed by the extraordinary achievement represented by her living in a fifty-room home filled with priceless art and antiques that are a wonder for others to behold. At the same time, it is a telling facet of Sophia's humanity that she knows that the hard work she has put into her career creates a kinship with people who lead very different lives.

OPPOSITE: At The Museum of Modern Art, New York, in 1966, Loren attended the opening of an exhibition of photographs of her in her various films. For the event, she was bedecked with chunky jewelry and a breathy, white, flowered Dior.

As a public figure becomes a beloved celebrity, the public clamors to see more of the star's personal side. While Loren opened herself up to the public through her relationships with photographers, she also obliged her adoring fans by hosting a number of television specials that invited the audience into her life.

One such special was *Sophia Loren in Rome*, which aired on ABC in November 1964. The producers, Phil D'Antoni and Norman Baer, had approached Sophia with the understanding that the content of the special would be Loren's own insights and feelings about the magnificent city.

In *Sophia Loren in Rome*, the captivating star wears four different couture outfits from Marc Bohan's autumn Dior collection. She graduates from fantasy figure—even from internationally acclaimed actor—to chic, worldly Italian hostess, armed with fresh and personable commentary about the ancient city—*her* Rome. Loren engages the viewer directly, making eye contact with the camera; the effect is almost Brechtian after her films. Her attire is sleek, modern, somewhat unconstructed, and in neutral tones, while her hair is styled in the same minimalist black bob she wears in *Five Miles to Midnight* (1961).

Sophia went on to host other television specials, including *With Love, Sophia*. The show, which aired on ABC on October 25, 1967, was an ambitious musical fantasy that centered on the Villa Ponti. In keeping with her then diva status, special billboard-size Avedon fashion images of Loren were erected in the garden as scenic elements. Tony Bennett sang some of the numbers on the soundtrack and Loren sang three herself.

In the decades following these spectaculars, Loren went on to utilize television in her creative endeavors, both as a promotional tool and as a means of delivering entertainment and content to a far-reaching audience. Through television, she advertised both her perfume, Sophia, and her Zyloware eyeglasses in the 1980s; she even appeared in 1998 on QVC to sell her cookbook *Sophia Loren's Recipes & Memories*. On the entertainment side, she starred in a number of television movies, including *Sophia Loren: Her Own Story* (1980), in which she turned in riveting performances as both herself and her mother— once again demonstrating her tremendous versatility. In recent years, she has continued to radiate from television screens across the world, both as an interviewee and as a magnificent presence at the Academy Awards.

A B O V E : This elegant image of Loren, demonstrating the eloquence of her Neapolitan gestures, appeared on the cover of *TV Magazine* in November 1964 to promote her special *Sophia Loren in Rome*.

Which comes first: becoming an icon, or being recognized as one? In 1991, Loren received both an honorary César (France's Oscar) for lifetime achievement and an honorary Oscar as "one of the genuine treasures of world cinema." In 1994, she was awarded a Silver Bear by the Berlin Film Festival for lifetime achievement; the following year she received, from the Hollywood Foreign Press Association, the Cecil B. DeMille Award for service to filmmaking. Her 1998 Golden Lion from the Venice Film Festival and 1999 David di Donatello Award (Italy's Oscar) both recognized her career achievement. For her generosity outside the world of cinema, Loren received in 1996 a NATO/ShoWest award for lifetime achievement. This accolade no doubt took into consideration her work on behalf of the National Alliance for the Prevention of Child Abuse and Maltreatment—in honor of which she was invited by President Jimmy Carter to the White House in 1980—as well as her long service to the United Nations as goodwill ambassador and spokesperson. The new millennium will doubtless bring more honors for her professional and humanitarian achievements.

Loren's lack of award snobbery is pronounced—she graciously acknowledges the plaudits of fans outside the U.S.–Western Europe film axis. In 1999, for example, she traveled to the Slovak Republic to accept a lifetime achievement award at the seventh annual Trenčíanske Teplice Art Film Festival. Thousands of onlookers thronged the spa town's streets to glimpse Sophia Loren as she addressed her audience. As she held her award, she proclaimed, "This will take a place next to my Oscar." The crowd cheered her adoringly.

*S*ophia Loren's is a rich and complex personality. With all her professional rigor, she does not allow herself to be imprisoned by the public perception that she has deliberately invented. She refuses to take her image too seriously, that is, to treat the icon she has created as something brittle, and this has no doubt contributed to the longevity of that image. She is devoted to her family, and her sons and niece Alessandra have appeared onscreen with her; she vacations with her sister, Maria, and when she visits Pozzuoli (as she recently did while filming *Francesca e Nunziata* [2000] nearby), she causes a press circus almost akin to a papal appearance.

Loren complements unmatched diva magnificence with an equally well-publicized enjoyment of hands-on, traditionally female areas such as cooking and makeup. In her 1984 book, *Women & Beauty*, which is in some ways more revealing than her official autobiography, *Sophia Living and Loving: Her Own Story*, Loren proposes that exercising control is a way of achieving tranquillity. She advises being clear about what is within your control and striving for the feeling of security that prevails when everything is well in hand. She begins the book with a

OPPOSITE: Twinkle, twinkle lovely star . . . Valentino's drop-dead shimmering lace gown for Loren's 1991 honorary Oscar was accessorized with powerfully large earrings—and a beaming face that dominated even the jewels.

discussion of her most notable quality: discipline. Loren is always open to learning; Marc Bohan describes this trait as her "special intelligence." She is notoriously punctual and well informed about whatever proceedings she is engaged in, and she trusts her excellent instincts.

True to form, she recommends in *Women & Beauty* that women be aware and responsible, defying conventional Hollywood wisdom. She writes, "If you can learn to use your mind as well as your powder puff, you will become more truly beautiful." Except for a minor pre-Hollywood slimming in 1957, her celebrated measurements seem to have remained about the same, as she quickly regained her figure after her two sedentary pregnancies. Her regimen includes a forty-five-minute walk every day. Loren has publicly criticized the film world's double standard regarding older actresses and actors. She herself is aging gracefully and gradually: she is a splendid woman of a certain age, an example of self-possession and identity.

In a personal communication with the author, Gianfranco Ferré summed up the Loren mystique by challenging it:

Sophia Loren's beauty is indisputable, but that's surely not the only reason for her popularity. Speaking about Sophia Loren, I've often happened to call her "the last true diva," in the best sense of the word: a great actress who is also a wonderful woman, sweet and strong, rich in temperament, intelligent, witty, fun— qualities which, moreover, are reflected in her talent and in her performances. Sophia isn't loved because she is beautiful. She is loved because she's real.

An icon is a conflation of resources and authors, wrapped in fantasy. Sophia Loren is at the same time Sofia Scicolone, teenage beauty contestant; Sofia Lazzaro, *fumetti* vamp; Carlo's companion and wife of four decades; *Mamma*, the beaming mother of two handsome, hard-won sons; and the aproned kitchen doyenne of cookbooks. She is at once the most magnificent, most down-to-earth, and most elusive of stars. For every film role she plays, she calls upon some aspect of her imagination, intelligence, and compassion, and this reaching within, in turn, has made her an extraordinarily full person. In the end, her greatest talent may be her continual self-creation, fueled by her boundless, striding energy and curiosity. One always imagines her smiling, with a smile that expresses warmth and gently ironic amusement at the human comedy. Perhaps, when all is said and done, the secret of Sophia's style is not that she is larger than life, but that she is as large as life.

OPPOSITE: The vivacious superstar, in 1999, seems to be set aglow by the mere proximity of cameras. This is the smile and the tossed-back mane of a seasoned professional.

selected bibliography

Bardin, Brantley. "Sophia So Fierce." *Details*, January 1996.

Benevy, Robert. "Sophia's American 'Desire.'" *New York Mirror Magazine*, November 10, 1957.

Bohan, Marc. Telephone interviews with author, November 24, 27–28, 2000.

Bruzzi, Stella. *Undressing Cinema: Clothing and Identity in the Movies*. New York: Routledge, 1997.

Collins, Nancy. "Sophia: The Immaculate Siren." *Vanity Fair*, January 1991.

Crawley, Tony. *The Films of Sophia Loren*. Secaucus, N.J.: Citadel Press, 1976, 1979.

De Sica, Vittorio. "De Sica on Sophia Loren." *Vogue*, November 15, 1962.

Ferré, Gianfranco. Fax interview with author, December 2000.

Fiori, Pamela. "Sophia." *Town & Country*, January 2000.

Fuller, Graham. "Sofia Scicolone (Sophia Loren)." *Interview*, October 1993.

Hamblin, Dora Jane. "Carlo and Sophia." *Life*, September 18, 1964.

Hammill, Pete. "Sophia Loren: First, I Am a Woman." *Saturday Evening Post*, February 15, 1964.

Hardy, Steven. "Oh, La Loren." *Gazette* (Montreal), October 18, 1998.

Harris, Warren G. *Sophia Loren: A Biography*. New York: Simon & Schuster, 1998.

Hershey, Lenore. "Sophia: Serenely Female." *Ladies' Home Journal*, January 1971.

Hotchner, A. E. *Sophia Living and Loving: Her Own Story*. New York: William Morrow, 1979.

"Italy's Sophia Loren: A New Star—A 'Mount Vesuvius.'" *Newsweek*, August 15, 1955.

Judge, Frank. "Patience Is Her Middle Name in Sophia's Toughest Role." *TV Magazine*, November 8–14, 1964.

Kirby, Heather. "Sophia Loren at Sixty." *Ladies' Home Journal*, August 1994.

Kolthow, Barry. "For Sophia Loren, Beauty's All in the Head." *New Orleans Times-Picayune*, December 22, 1995.

Levy, Alan. *Forever, Sophia: An Intimate Portrait*. New York: St. Martin's Press, 1979, 1986.

Loren, Sophia. "A Hollywood vivo così: Quaderno segreto di Sophia Loren." *Epoca*, October 20, 1957.

———. *In the Kitchen with Love*. Garden City, N.Y.: Doubleday & Co., 1972.

———. "Sophia Loren Discusses Her Life," interview by Barbara Walters, *Barbara Walters Special*, ABC, September 12, 2000.

———. *Sophia Loren's Recipes & Memories*. New York: GT Publishing, 1998.

———. *Women & Beauty*. New York: William Morrow & Co., 1984.

Loren, Sophia, and Romilda Villani. "Sophia Loren and Her Mother." *Ladies' Home Journal*, October 1974.

Masi, Stefano, and Enrico Lancia. *Italian Movie Goddesses: Over 80 of the Greatest Women in Italian Cinema*. Rome: Gremese International s.r.l., 1997.

Maza, Cristina. "Il grande ritorno di Sofia." *Chi*, November 29, 2000.

McPhee, John. "Much Woman." *Time*, April 6, 1962.

Moravia, Alberto. "This Is Your Life, Sophia Loren." *Show*, September 1962.

Mormorio, Diego. *Tazio Secchiaroli:*

Greatest of the Paparazzi, trans. Alexandra Bonfante-Warren. New York: Harry N. Abrams, 1999.

Moscati, Italo. *Sophia Loren: tutto cominciò quando la madre di una ragazza di Pozzuoli sognò di diventare Greta Garbo*. Venezia: Marsilio, 1994.

Negulesco, Jean. *Things I Did . . . and Things I Think I Did*. New York: Linden Press, 1984.

Newmark, Judith. "Hepburn and Loren: Getting Down to Earth." *St. Louis Post-Dispatch*, September 20, 1995.

Oppenheimer, Peer J. "Sophia Loren's Advice: Make Your Faults Your Virtues!" *Family Weekly*, November 10, 1963.

———. "Big Things Coming from Hollywood!" *Family Weekly*, September 9, 1956.

Peer, Robert. "Sophia Loren Says, 'I'm Glad I Married Carlo.'" *Silver Screen*, February 1960.

"Le prime scene a colori di 'Filumena Marturano.'" *Oggi*, April 23, 1964.

Rooney, David. "From Pin-Up to Decorated Thesp, Loren Lionized." *Variety*, August 31, 1998.

Rosen, Marjorie. "Some Spicy Meatball." *New York Times Magazine*, November 24, 1996.

Russell, William. "Loren: A Long Distance Stunner." *Herald* (Glasgow), September 19, 1994.

Seligson, Tom. "Sophia Loren Has a Secret." *Parade*, January 18, 1987.

Shaw, Sam. *Sophia Loren in the Camera Eye*. New York: An Exeter Book, 1979.

"Sophia Loren racconta la sua vita." *Oggi*, February 14, 1957.

"Sophia Loren's Dos by the Dozens." *HairDo*, Special International Edition, January 1963.

Steelman, Ben. "Oscar's Love for Loren Expressed with Award." *Toronto Star*, February 26, 1991.

Stern, Michael. "Carlo Ponti's Work of Art." *Cosmopolitan*, November 1962.

"Ten Best Dressed: Sophia Loren." *People Weekly*, September 20, 1999.

Terry, Clifford. "Sophia's Satisfied: After Nearly 100 Films, Loren Takes the Bad with the Good." *Chicago Tribune*, October 7, 1990.

Turner, Jim. "Sophia's Choice." *Detour*, December 1994.

"The Way I Looked That Night: Stars Retrace the (Sometimes Bumpy) Path to the Red Carpet." *People Weekly*, April 10, 2000.

Whitcomb, Jon. "Sophia Loren in America." *Cosmopolitan*, February 1958.

Williams, Christian. "The Glory of Rome: The Three Faces of Sophia Loren." *Washington Post*, October 25, 1980.

Zec, Donald. *Sophia: An Intimate Biography*. New York: David McKay Company, Inc., 1975.

selected filmography

Note: All dates are dates of film production, not of release. Films are listed in chronological order of production. Names of major studios are given in studio-produced vehicles, and producers are individually named where studios are lacking. This list is by no means comprehensive of Loren's oeuvre; it includes only titles cited in the book.

Quo Vadis? (1950). MGM. Dir. Mervyn LeRoy. Uncredited appearance.

Africa sotto i mari (*Africa Under the Seas*; *Woman of the Red Sea*, 1952). Titanus-Phoenix Film. Dir. Giovanni Roccardi. Sophia Loren [First film credit with this name] as Barbara.

Aïda (1953). Oscar Film. Dir. Clemente Fracassi. Sophia Loren [with Renata Tebaldi's voice] as Aïda.

Tempi nostri (*The Anatomy of Love*; *Our Times*, 1953). Lux Film. Dir. Alessandro Blasetti. Sophia Loren as The Girl.

Due notti con Cleopatra (*Two Nights with Cleopatra*, 1953). Excelsa-Rosa Film. Dir. Mario Mattoli. Sophia Loren as Cleopatra and Nisca.

Attila, flagello di Dio (*Attila*; *Attila, Scourge of God*; *Attila, Wrath of God*; *Attila the Hun*, 1953). Ponti–De Laurentiis/Lux Film. Dir. Pietro Francisci. Sophia Loren as Honoria.

L'oro di Napoli (*The Gold of Naples*, 1954). Ponti–De Laurentiis. Dir. Vittorio De Sica. Sophia Loren as Sofia.

La donna del fiume (*Woman of the River*, 1954). Ponti–De Laurentiis/Excelsa/Centaur Film. Dir. Mario Soldati. Sophia Loren as Nives Mongolini.

Peccato che sia una canaglia (*Too Bad She's Bad*, 1954). Documento Film. Dir. Alessandro Blasetti. Sophia Loren as Lina.

Il segno di Venere (*The Sign of Venus*, 1955). Titanus Film. Dir. Dino Risi. Sophia Loren as Agnese.

La bella mugnaia (*The Miller's Beautiful Wife*, 1955). Ponti–De Laurentiis/Titanus Film. Dir. Mario Camerini. Sophia Loren as Carmela.

Pane, amore e . . . (*Scandal in Sorrento*; *Bread, Love and . . .*, 1955). Titanus/S.G.C. Films. Dir. Dino Risi. Sophia Loren as Donna Sofia.

La fortuna di essere donna (*Lucky to Be a Woman*; *What a Woman!*, 1955). Documento/Le Louvre Films. Dir. Alessandro Blasetti. Sophia Loren as Antoinette Fallari.

The Pride and the Passion (1956). United Artists. Prod.-Dir. Stanley Kramer. Sophia Loren as Juana [Loren's first English-speaking role].

Boy on a Dolphin (1956). 20th Century Fox. Dir. Jean Negulesco. Sophia Loren as Phaedra.

Legend of the Lost (1957). United Artists/Batjac Productions/Dear Film. Prod.-Dir. Henry Hathaway. Sophia Loren as Dita.

Desire Under the Elms (1957). Paramount. Dir. Delbert Mann. Sophia Loren as Anna Cabot.

Houseboat (1957). Paramount. Dir. Melville Shavelson. Sophia Loren as Cinzia Zaccardi.

The Key (1957). Columbia. Dir. Carol Reed. Sophia Loren as Stella.

filmography (continued)

The Black Orchid (1958). Paramount. Dir. Martin Ritt. Sophia Loren as Rose Bianco.

That Kind of Woman (1958). Paramount. Dir. Sidney Lumet. Sophia Loren as Kay.

Heller in Pink Tights (1959). Paramount. Dir. George Cukor. Sophia Loren as Angela Rossini.

A Breath of Scandal (1959). Paramount. Dir. Michael Curtiz. Sophia Loren as Princess Olympia.

It Started in Naples (1959). Paramount. Dir. Melville Shavelson. Sophia Loren as Lucia Curcio.

The Millionairess (1960). 20th Century Fox. Dir. Anthony Asquith. Sophia Loren as Epifania Parerga.

La ciociara (*Two Women*, 1960). Champion Film/Les Films Marceau/Cocinor. Dir. Vittorio De Sica. Sophia Loren as Cesira.

El Cid (1960). Dear Film. Dir. Anthony Mann. Sophia Loren as Jimena/Chimene.

"The Lottery." Dir. Vittorio De Sica. From *Boccaccio '70* (1961). Carlo Ponti. Sophia Loren as Zoe.

Madame Sans-Gêne (*Madame*, 1961). Carlo Ponti. Dir. Christian Jaque. Sophia Loren as Caroline Huebscher.

Five Miles to Midnight (1961). United Artists/Filmsonor/Dear Film. Prod.-Dir. Anatole Litvak. Sophia Loren as Lisa Macklin.

Ieri, oggi e domani (*Yesterday, Today and Tomorrow*, 1962). Carlo Ponti/Joseph E. Levine. Dir. Vittorio De Sica. Sophia Loren as Adelina Sbaratti, Anna Molteni, Mara.

The Fall of the Roman Empire (1963). Paramount/Samuel Bronston/Rank Organisation/Roma Film. Dir. Anthony Mann. Sophia Loren as Lucilla.

Matrimonio all'italiana (*Marriage, Italian-Style*, 1964). Carlo Ponti/Joseph E. Levine. Prod.-Dir. Vittorio De Sica. Sophia Loren as Filumena Marturano.

Lady L (1965). Carlo Ponti/MGM. Dir. Peter Ustinov. Sophia Loren as Louise, Lady L.

Arabesque (1965). Universal. Prod.-Dir. Stanley Donen. Sophia Loren as Yasmin Azir.

A Countess from Hong Kong (1966). Universal. Dir.-Screenwriter Charles Chaplin. Sophia Loren as Natascha.

C'era una volta (*More Than a Miracle*; *Happily Ever After*; *Cinderella, Italian Style*, 1966). Carlo Ponti/M.G.M. Dir. Francesco Rosi. Sophia Loren as Isabella.

I girasoli (*Sunflower*, 1969). Carlo Ponti/Joseph E. Levine/Arthur Cohn. Dir. Vittorio De Sica. Sophia Loren as Giovanna.

Bianco, rosso e . . . (*The White Sister*; *The Sin*, 1971). Carlo Ponti. Dir. Alberto Lattuada. Sophia Loren as Sister Germana.

La mortadella (*Lady Liberty*, 1971). Carlo Ponti/Warner Bros./United Artists. Dir. Mario Monacelli. Sophia Loren as Maddalena Ciarrapico.

Man of La Mancha (1972). United Artists. Prod.-Dir. Arthur Hiller. Sophia Loren as Aldonza/Dulcinea.

The Voyage (1973). United Artists/Carlo Ponti. Dir. Vittorio De Sica. Sophia Loren as Adriana De Mauro.

Le testament (*Jury of One*; *The Verdict*, 1974). Carlo Ponti. Dir. André Cayatte. Sophia Loren as Teresa Leoni.

Brief Encounter (1974). Television movie. NBC/Hallmark Hall of Fame. Dir. Alan Bridges. Sophia Loren as Anna Jesson.

Una giornata particolare (*A Special Day*, 1975). Carlo Ponti. Dir. Ettore Scola. Sophia Loren as Antonietta.

The Cassandra Crossing (1976). Carlo Ponti/Lew Grade. Dir. George Pan Cosmatos. Sophia Loren as Jennifer Rispoli Chamberlain.

Fatto di sangue fra due uomini per causa di una vedova (*Blood Feud*; *Revenge*, 1978). Warner Bros. Prod.-Dir. Lina Wertmüller. Sophia Loren as Titina Paterno.

Sophia Loren: Her Own Story (1980). Television movie. Alex Ponti. Dir. Mel Stuart. Sophia Loren as Romilda Villani and herself.

Sabato, domenica e lunedi (*Saturday, Sunday and Monday*, 1990). Carlo Ponti/Alex Ponti/Reteitalia/Silvio Berlusconi. Dir. Lina Wertmüller. Sophia Loren as Rosa Priori.

Prêt-à-Porter (*Ready to Wear*, 1994). Miramax. Prod.-Dir. Robert Altman. Sophia Loren as Isabella de la Fontaine.

Grumpier Old Men (1995). Warner Bros./Lancaster Gate. Dir. Howard Deutch. Sophia Loren as Maria Ragetti.

Francesca e Nunziata (2000). Prod.-Dir. Lina Wertmüller. Forthcoming as of printing. Sophia Loren as Francesca.

index

Academy Awards, 5, 28, 40, 77, 90, 95, 101, 110
Aïda (1953), 14, 27, 60
Altman, Robert, 6, 90
The Anatomy of Love (1953), 59
Antonioni, Michelangelo, 90, 104
Arabesque (1965), *4*, 5, 78, *79*, 81, 82, 85
Armani, Giorgio, 77, 95, 97
Attila (1953), 60
Avedon, Richard, 5, 89, 107

Balenciaga, Cristóbal, 85
Barr, Neil, 5, 89, 107
La bella mugnaia (1955), *16*, 17, 93
Bianco, rosso e... (1971), 98, 101
The Black Orchid (1958), 36, *37*, 39
Blood Feud (1978), 44, 86
Bluebeard's Seven Wives (1950), 56
Boccaccio '70 (1961), 18, *19*, 66
Bohan, Marc, 5, 17, *76*, 77, 78, 81, 82, 86, 90, 108, 112
Boyer, Charles, *58*, 59, 77
Boy on a Dolphin (1956), 22, 24, *25*, *25*, 77
Brando, Marlon, 81
A Breath of Scandal (1959), *70*, 73, 85
Burton, Richard, 46, 89

The Cassandra Crossing (1976), 78, 82
Castet, Frédéric, *84*, 85, 101
C'era una volta (1966), *12*, 13, 18
Chaplin, Charlie, 81
La ciociara (1960), 28, *30*, 31, 35, 43, 89, 101
Costumes, 43, 63. *See also* Wardrobes
historical, 46
intimate, 66–67
peasant, 17, 18, 21, 24, 27, 28, *29*
romantic, *26*, 27
Victorian, 64
western, 27
wet, 24, *25*, *25*
A Countess from Hong Kong (1966), 78, 81, 86

Cukor, George, 63
De Laurentiis, Dino, 2, 17
De Sica, Vittorio, 14, 17, 18, 24, 28, 36, 39, 40, 43, 46, 57, 60, 69, 89, 101
Desire Under the Elms (1957), 22, *26*, 27, 45
Dior, Christian, 17, 74, 77, 86
Donen, Stanley, 78
La donna del fiume (1954), 21, 22, 23, 24
Due notti con Cleopatra (1953), 60, 62, 63

Eisenstaedt, Alfred, 66, 107
El Cid (1960), 28, 45
Escoffier, Marcel, 18, 46, 66, 67
Eyeglass line, 6, 7, 108

The Fall of the Roman Empire (1963), 28
Fatto di sangue fra due uomini per causa di una vedova (1978), 44, 86
Fellini, Federico, 18, 90, 104
Ferragamo, Salvatore, 77
Ferré, Gianfranco, 6, 90, 94, 95, 112
Five Miles to Midnight (1961), 107, 108
Fontana Sorelle, 73, 74
La fortuna di essere donna (1955), 58, 59, 74
Francesca e Nunziata (2000), 44, 67, 110
Fumetti, 56, 57, 60, 63, 102

Gable, Clark, 39
The Gold of Naples (1954), 14, 17, 24
Grant, Cary, 27, 39, 64, 101
Grumpier Old Men (1995), 6

Hairstyles, 28, 43, 44–45
Head, Edith, 27, 36, 63, 64, *65*
Hearts at Sea (1950), 56
Heller in Pink Tights (1959), 36, 44, 63, 64, *65*, 85
Holden, William, 64
Houseboat (1957), 27, 36, 39

Ieri, oggi e domani (1962), 40, 64, 66, *68*, 69, 82, *83*, 92

I girasoli (1969), 32, 35, 42, 43, 69
In the Kitchen with Love, 49
It Started in Naples (1959), 38, 39, 85

Jeakins, Dorothy, 27

The Key (1957), 64
King, Bill, 89, 107
Kramer, Stanley, 27

Lady L (1965), 40, 44, 46, 67, 107
Lagerfeld, Karl, 85
Laroche, Guy, 85
Legend of the Lost (1957), 64
Lemmon, Jack, 6
Lucky to Be a Woman (1955), 58, 59, 74

Madame Sans-Gêne (1961), 18, 44, 46, 67
Makeup, 27, 28, 31, 43
Man of La Mancha (1972), 20, 21
Marriage, Italian-Style (1964), 39, 60, 66, 67, 69, 104
Mastroianni, Marcello, 17, 39, 40, *41*, 43, 46, 57, 60, *61*, 64, 66, 69, *83*, 104
Matrimonio all'italiana (1964), 39, 60, 66, 67, 69, 104
Matthau, Walter, 6
The Miller's Beautiful Wife (1955), *16*, 17, 93
The Millionairess (1960), 85, 93
Moravia, Alberto, 28, 35, 36, 50, 82
More Than a Miracle (1966), *12*, 13, 18

Negulesco, Jean, 22, 24, 25, 59, 77

O'Neill, Eugene, 22, 27
L'oro di Napoli (1954), 14, 17, 24

Pane, amore e... (1955), 17, 24
Peccato che sia una canaglia (1954), 59, 60, *61*
Peck, Gregory, 78, 81
Penn, Irving, 5, 89, 107
Ponti, Carlo, 2, 13, 14, *15*, 21, 43, 49, 55, 56, 57, 59, 60, 74, 86, 89, 101, 104

index (continued)

Ponti, Carlo Jr., 2, 3, 40, 43
Ponti, Edoardo, 2, 40, 104
Prêt-à-Porter (1994), 5, 6, 64, 69, 90, 93, 93, 95
The Pride and the Passion (1956), 27, 28, 39, 52, 55, 104

Quinn, Anthony, 36
Quo Vadis? (1950), 2, 56

Ready to Wear (1994), 5, 6, 64, 69, 90, 93, 93, 95
Roles
    comedy, 14, 35, 59, 60, 64
    couture, 72–97
    dramatic, 21, 35
    earth-mother, 32–50
    peasant, 17, 18, 21, 28, 29
    political, 46
    sensual, 54–69
    wet, 24, 25, 25

Sabato, domenica e lunedi (1990), 49
Sabbatini, Enrico, 43, 46
Saint Laurent, Yves, 77
Saturday, Sunday and Monday (1990), 49
Scandal in Sorrento (1955), 17, 24
Schuberth, Emilio, 74
Scicolone, Riccardo, 1

Secchiaroli, Tazio, 5, 9, 43, 66, 101, 104
Shaw, Sam, 5, 49, 104
The Sign of Venus (1955), 59
Sinatra, Frank, 27
Snowdon, Lord, 2, 13, 35, 107
Sophia Living and Loving: Her Own Story, 2, 40, 110
Sophia Loren's Recipes & Memories, 49, 108
Sordi, Alberto, 62, 63
A Special Day (1975), 46
Sunflower (1969), 32, 35, 42, 43, 69

Taylor, Elizabeth, 89
Television specials, 5, 6, 46, 78, 108–109
Tempi nostri (1953), 59
Too Bad She's Bad (1954), 59, 60, 61
Two Nights with Cleopatra (1953), 60, 62, 63
Two Women (1960), 28, 30, 31, 35, 43, 89, 101

Una giornata particolare (1975), 46
Ustinov, Peter, 40

Valentino, Mario, 77
The Verdict (1974), 78, 82
Villani, Romilda, 1, 35, 56
Visconti, Luchino, 18

Vivier, Roger, 78
The Voyage (1973), 46, 47, 67, 89
Vreeland, Diana, 5, 44, 89

Wardrobes, 72–97
    Armani, 77, 95, 97
    Balmain, 86, 87
    couture, 72–97
    Dior, 74, 76, 77, 78, 79, 80, 81, 82, 83, 85, 86, 90, 94, 94, 95, 100, 101, 106, 107, 108
    footwear, 77, 78
    furs, 84, 85, 100, 101
    hats, 90, 92–93
    historical, 60
    Schuberth, 74, 75
    sensual, 59
    Valentino, ix, 89, 90, 91, 110, 111
Wayne, John, 64
Wertmüller, Lina, 44, 49, 67, 86
The White Sister (1971), 98, 101
Woman of the River (1954), 21, 22, 23, 24

Yesterday, Today and Tomorrow (1962), 40, 64, 66, 68, 69, 82, 83, 92

photo credits

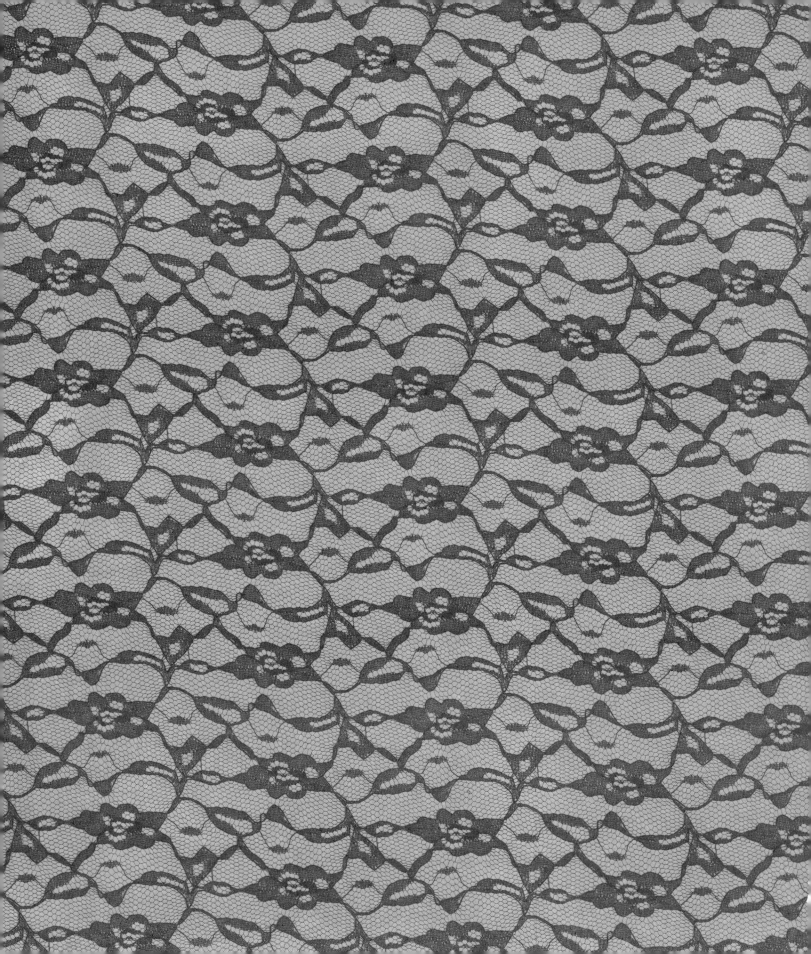